The Lion's Roar

A Prophetic Wakeup Call

John Caldwell

© John Caldwell 2020

"Unless otherwise indicated, all Scripture quotations are from The ESV® Bible (The Holy Bible, English Standard Version®), copyright © 2001 by Crossway, a publishing ministry of Good News Publishers. Used by permission. All rights reserved."

*Front cover design by Mary Campagna Findley:
www.findleyfamilyvideopublications.com*

Endorsements

In *The Lion's Roar*, John Caldwell brings a timely challenge to the church in this hour! In his candid and forthright style, the author calls for a fresh examination of ourselves and our church practices, appealing for us to return to the Lord and seek Him with all our heart. While raising some big issues and concerns, the writer also pulls us forward in great hope for a reviving work of the Spirit and a great harvest of souls to the glory of Jesus Christ.

Steven Anderson, itinerant Apostle, and author of *Releasing Healing*.

I am reading this book in the midst of the Coronavirus Pandemic. It is a time of anxiety throughout the earth, but it is also a time of shaking in the Church, as old practices and ways of being and doing Church are not able to happen. In a time of shaking, the hope is that the foundations are secure. This book uncomfortable and powerfully begs the question, "Are they?" John presents us with some of the timeless truths of what it means to be God's people in the world and in doing so presents this current time as an opportunity to become more aligned to these truths. That alignment may mean that familiar ways of doing things may need to get left behind. Are we willing for that to be so, or do we long for a day when our churches can go back to business as usual?

Rev Kenny Borthwick, former leader of CLAN Gathering, Scotland.

'The Lion's Roar' is a compelling, confronting read and, perhaps, should carry a warning to the would-be reader 'Not for the Faint-Hearted'.

John has rightly perceived that an imbalance exists in the perspective of many in the modern church when it comes to core redemptive issues of grace and justice, love and judgement. He provides a biblical base for readers who deeply long for truth and are passionate about rebalancing a simplistic, unsatisfying, contemporary view and exchanging it for a profoundly biblical view.

'The Lion's Roar' draws upon, upon other inspirations, the journey of his own personal experience of conversion and his early development as a disciple of Jesus. It is readable, cogent, powerfully prophetic, diagnostic and corrective without condescension.

John is a gifted writer and captures the essential nature of his subject, the post-pandemic church. Touching the heart of his subject, as he has done in previous works, he does again in 'The Lion's Roar' which is 'Not for the Faint-Hearted'.

I commend it to you.

Timothy W. Jack, National Leader, Apostolic Church UK

This is definitely an 'in season' book for a Church and World seeking to grapple with and make sense of COVID-19. God is shaking the Nations ~ the author handles the subject matter re: the present crisis with wisdom and sensitivity. He answers the key question ~ what is God saying right now?

Praise the Lord for his Church but the hard truth we have been struggling to accept in the U.K is it's an ageing church with many branches withering into decline altogether! Our response to this has often been to rehash 1980's / 1990's style activities and give them a new name! John outlines God's response ~ a wake-up call and a prophetic outline of God's priorities for the Church in 21st Century. God is 'repurposing' both His Church and the Five Fold Ministry (Ephesians 4:11) Gifts to facilitate this.

We need to hear the cry and call of God in our own hearts and then migrate to new Kingdom positions away from old and obsolete positions we occupied historically. The author correctly identifies God's 'How' and 'Why' to initiate and complete the process of 21st century reformation and the harvest of souls we so eagerly desire to see.

This book is neither a devotional nor a typical 'end times' theology book! It's more like a 'tour guide' into a new era of Kingdom living. May we all experience the necessary 'Divine Confrontation' and appropriate 'Reset' in Christ Jesus to steward His contemporary plans for the United Kingdom and beyond.

Alan Ross, International Prophet, and Assistant Pastor at Gateway Church, Glasgow.

Written in the midst of an enforced wilderness experience for much of the world, I thought first of Isaiah chapter 41:18:

"I will make the wilderness a pool of water, and the dry land springs of water." Out of a wilderness the author exposes a pool of water and a refreshing spring of water. I doubt everyone will get what he is saying. The lion is roaring and many are asking, what's that awful noise? As it says on the cover: *A Prophetic Wakeup Call*. I hope as you read this book you will wake up and realise the reality that the church has been sound asleep living, not in some idyllic dream land (which would be bad), but in the nightmare condition of complacency. To cut to the chase, only read this if you are prepared to rise from your slumbers. It's a call and a warning.

Pastor, Eric Scott, Perth Elim.

Prophets were never born for times of peace and tranquility. They were born for adversity. They are the 'Jeremiahs' that often prophesy from prison cells as the shadow of war and persecution loom. They are the 'Elijahs' in drought and the 'Josephs' in famine. This book, this outcry, is one of those: a voice crying in the wilderness of post-modern religion, turning over tables to make a way for the Lord. True prophets will always fight for the poor and preach the Gospel to them as well. They are for the underdog, the outliers and the outcasts. They can't be bought. This book and its author are optic to what is coming — a new breed.

Chad Taylor, Consuming Fire Ministries, and author of *Why Revival Still Tarries.*

Acknowledgements

A huge thanks to Eric Scott for editing the chapters – almost as quickly as I wrote them! This process has been a lot smoother thanks to your help. Thanks also to Steven Anderson, and Angela Holtz Loaiza, for also helping with the editing process – it's greatly appreciated. Thanks also to Alistair Matheson – your constructive feedback has helped me soften some of the blunt edges. Like-wise Steven Anderson also provided some constructive criticism. Thank you to everyone who endorsed the book – your bravery knows no bounds! And as ever, eternal thanks to my wife Laura who has had to live with me whilst I wrote a book in three days – not easy in a small house, with kids, during Lockdown. Finally, thank you to all the folks on social media who gave helpful feedback regarding the front cover. I hope you all like it! Finally, thank you Jesus, for your grace and mercy, and for the gift of writing. I pray this book brings you glory, edifies your church, and reaches the lost.

Contents

Foreword	9
Introduction	12
1. The Cry of the Prophets	24
2. A Warning of Judgement	37
3. A Call to Repentance	47
4. The Fear of the Lord	58
5. A Re-aligned Church	69
6. The Coming Harvest	81
7. Rescue the Lost	91
8. A Baptism of the Holy Spirit & Fire	105
9. Resurrecting the Crucified Life	118
10. Restoring the Gifts	128
11. Worshipping the Lion-Like Lamb	141
12. A Vision of the Return of Christ	153

Foreword

John Caldwell had his dark locks shorn not that long ago. Gone are both the lion's mane and an uncanny resemblance (for those old enough to remember) to Keith Green. But the new cut is no disguise. So let me say before you open the first page: you can judge *this* book by its cover!

Is this man a prophet? Is he an evangelist … or a teacher?

Lions don't fit into boxes! I see John as a modern-day Stephen, untitled, passionate, untamed in spirit and untempered in speech, articulate, offensive, young yet battle scarred, but fortunate to live in an age when you don't get dragged out and stoned any more.

But there was something else I was going to add about him … What was it, again? Oh yes – he speaks a lot of truth!

And if he is for some too hot to handle, that puts him in good company! How many of today's user-friendly churches would Stephen, Paul or John the Baptist – I'm being kind and missing out *The* Name – be welcome in, with their unmodified, confrontative, corrective language?

Some, like I, will raise an amen at various points. But don't get too cocky – you'll be next! But if you're willing to take it on the chin, you'll make it to the last chapter. Most reassuringly, this is also the attitude of the ex-pugilist who wrote this book, as he demonstrated through his own recent admission, "People aren't getting healed by *my* shadow yet either!"

When you get into the substance of John's message, you'll be stirred by irrefutable biblical truth. John takes us back to the DNA of church in true world-changing mode: bold proclamation of a Gospel of righteousness, and the unquenchable power of a Holy Spirit Who does His own convincing.

And in the midst of it all, an uncompromising church, stirred from its slumber by the roar of men like piano-stool prophet Keith Green – and here's a quote I'm surprised John didn't select – "The world is sleeping in the dark, that the church just can't fight, 'cos it's asleep ... in the light."

I cannot ask you to 'enjoy' a book whose cry is, "Waken up!"

But I do pray it will stir many to get up, get dressed and get going!

Alistair, J. Matheson, Senior pastor, Glasgow City Church

"This is what the LORD says to me: "As a lion growls, a great lion over its prey— and though a whole band of shepherds is called together against it, it is not frightened by their shouts or disturbed by their clamour— so the LORD Almighty will come down to do battle on Mount Zion and on its heights."
Isaiah 31:4

The attacks of the enemy will stand still at one sound of the roar from the Lion of Judah! Let the lion arise within you. Let Him live. Let Him arise, conquer the things that are holding you back and establish the Kingdom of God in your realm of influence.
Patricia King

Introduction

The world is undergoing a major shaking. The discovery of a new virus "Covid19" has brought the world to a halt. Governments, in an attempt to slow the spread of the virus have placed society on lockdown. Everyone has been told to stay at home, all non-essential businesses have been closed, and all social gatherings have been banned. We are only allowed to leave our homes for essential food, medicine, to help a vulnerable person, or for exercise once a day. Parks are shut, restaurants are shut, cinemas are shut, pubs are shut, schools are shut, and churches are shut. Life as we knew is shut. In terms of global events, this is massive. In addition to the global rising death toll from the virus itself, there is the fact that the economy is being shaken. Then there are the rumblings behind the scene between global powers. The US and China, in particular, are flexing their muscles like two heavyweight boxers at a championship weigh in. Tensions are rising. The nations are being shaken, but is the church waking up, or are we still sleeping? The Lion is roaring, but are we snoring? Now is not the time to hit the snooze button.

Of course, I'm not saying the church is completely inactive – the church is always active to some degree. Nor am I implying every part of the body of Christ is asleep – there are many who are awake. I'm not even suggesting that I'm fully awake. I too need to awaken to the fullness of God's purpose and power. I too am in need of deep, daily repentance.

Many church leaders have demonstrated how innovative and adaptable they are by their swift ability to learn quickly how to utilise modern technology in order to keep in contact with their flock, get the word of God out via live stream, and take their small groups online via conference call software packages such as Zoom. But that is not my point. The church has always demonstrated its evolutionary prowess. Its ability to adapt to changing seasons is the reason why it has survived thousands of years of cultural shifts, revolutions, natural disasters, world wars and pandemics. The church knows how to adapt. But adapting to changing circumstances is not the same as hearing what the Lord is saying in the midst of shifting seasons. The church is certainly in survival mode, but it's not yet in revival mode!

In fact, survival mode is a hindrance to revival. In times of great shaking, God is dismantling and stripping back all that hinders. When we are in survival mode, we often desperately seek to cling on to the very structures, programs and approaches that God is stripping from us. We see this in scripture often. When God was about to strip the people of their temple and their land, the people were desperate to cling on to it. There were even 'prophets' who said everything was going to be fine. I mean surely God would never strip away essential things like the temple or the land? Undiscerning people always think like that. They can never see beyond the surface. Spiritual people on the other hand recognise that even good things can become the enemy of the best things. "Good" can get in the way of God. When God's gifts are more important than God, we have an idolatry problem, and God will strip away our idols in order to bring us to our senses.

A few weeks ago, the Lord gave me the following prophetic word:

> At the start of the year, many of us said the Lord was intending to lead us into 2020 vision. Maybe we've forgotten that in the midst of the current chaos. Or maybe we can't see how that can be true now. On the contrary: this season is exactly what the Lord is using to sharpen our sight.
>
> He is stripping away all the idols that have blinded us. He has removed the distractions. He is disciplining us. Pruning us for greater fruitfulness.
>
> How will we sharpen our sight?
>
> We must allow him to show us the areas in our lives that have been a hindrance. We must repent for our pursuit or acceptance of lesser things. We must surrender all competing loyalties. We must get the hidden sin out of our life.
>
> We must repent of prayerlessness.
>
> As we do this, we will start to discern the Lord and his purpose. As we fix our eyes on him, he will reveal his heart and his purpose. It's time to see, but we must be willing to go beyond where we are at in the present. This requires repentance from pride, and a baptism of humility. Some of us are still leaning on false crutches: theological

perspectives, denominational politics, and human wisdom—these things are a futile foundation. Those who rest on these will not be able to stand during the coming shaking that is coming upon the earth.

Wake up. Stir yourself. Pray. Ask the Lord to open up your eyes. Repent of your blindness. Receive eye salve that you may see. In these days, we need 2020 vision, or we will stumble and fall.

3rd April

On the 20th March, I posted the following status, which I also believe to be prophetic:

It's great that churches are live-streaming their services as an alternative since we have been told to shut down services. HOWEVER: if you are a family of believers and all you do is sit passively watching a live-stream service, you are missing God's purpose in this season. This is preparation ground for future persecution, and even future judgements. Even if you don't believe that, you should understand that you should be able to have church in your home, "where two or three are gathered."

That means, you should gather in a way that you can participate. Pray together. Read scripture together. Discuss the scriptures together. Break bread and share the cup together. YES YOU CAN DO THAT. You don't need a minister to have communion. You simply take bread, and grape juice and thank God for the cross. There is nothing magic about it. It's completely unbiblical to suggest that you need an ordained Minister in order to administer communion.

Are you on your own? Are you the only believer in your house? Break bread on your own or over Face Time with another believer.

Now is the time to learn to be the church outwith the institution.

The stabilisers are off the bike. It's time for you to learn to pedal and to free wheel.

Don't just settle for watching church services online. Get together in a video room with other believers if you are on your own. If you are a family of believers, actively study a passage of scripture. Make it creative and fun for the kids.

Allow room for various gifts to function.

You will be all the stronger for it.

Other people, many of them a lot more prophetic than I am, are saying similar things, On the 12th April 2020, prophet, and evangelist, Chad Taylor posted the following on Social Media:

3,000,000,000+ people (half the world) will never darken the door of a church, never view the live streaming multiplicity of Facebook videos, or buy the mountain of books. Yet, the western church still desperately, wildly, frantically attempts to climb back into broken cisterns, cracked wine-skins and tipped over salt shakers. For centuries following Pentecost in the Book of Acts buildings were obsolete. Early believers were scattered abroad preaching the Gospel and, "turned the world upside down..." For thousands of years Christians in foreign countries met anywhere that they safely could. To this day huts in far flung villages, basements in China, secret rendezvous points in North Korea. Along rivers, in deserts and even prison cells. Church couldn't be, never was, a building.

As Stephen faced the old guard of his day, declaring that it was never God's will to dwell in temples, houses and buildings — they stoned him. His courageous and prophetic message incited even Christ to stand up: "David found favor with God and asked for the privilege of building a permanent Temple for the God of Jacob. But it was Solomon who actually built it. However, the Most High doesn't live in temples made by human hands. As the prophet says, "'Heaven is my throne, and the earth is my footstool. What kind of house will you build for me, says the Lord, or what is the place of my rest?" (Acts 7:45-49) The threat to their systems, structures and systematic theology's dying was simply unbearable. They clasped their ears and gnashed their teeth.

I believe God will use every circumstance to get us out of our lazy pews, sleepy Sunday mornings and the endless cavalcade of conferences as He is now. The Book of Acts would be tucked nicely somewhere between 3rd John and Jude if they had never left the upper room. 26 chapters records their global exploits as God catapulted them from Jerusalem into Antioch and ultimately the uttermost parts of the earth. Friend, God has signed the death certificate already on today's broken structures and systems we call "church." With its outdated and outmoded methodology lacking any real mission. The burning question begging to be answered now is the same as it was 2000 years ago — will we stone Stephen too? Do we ignore the enormity of the hour and refuse to get out of the salt shaker and be the salt of the earth? The light of the world? Do we still obstinately force ourselves back into old wineskins and flawed ideologies that are often led by self-serving shepherds? God forbid! Or it will all be in vain!

My prayer today is this: that everything which is not of God, that has divorced itself from His ancient creed, "to go into all the world and preach the gospel to every creature," would die. A merciful death. A severe mercy. So that we can move on from the ashes and cinders of what was, that hardly ever worked anyways, into the rarefied air of a new beginning. A NEW DAY! The prophets of old stand at the banisters of eternity heralding the church of this hour but will we listen? "Forget the former things; do not dwell on the past. See, I am doing a new thing! Now it springs up; do you not perceive it? I am making a way in the wilderness and streams in the wasteland..." (Isaiah 43:18-19)

The Lion of the Tribe of Judah is roaring, but are we listening? There is a prophetic cry ringing out throughout the globe. That cry is an awakening cry. Are we listening? Or as Jesus often said, do we have "ears to hear, what the Spirit is saying to the churches?" This book is based on a few things, it is based on two key passages of scripture, and a prophetic poem that I wrote back in 2007. The scriptures use the imagery of the Lion roaring as a means of describing God's voice ringing out. It is a metaphor for the prophetic call of God.

This prophetic call has three main elements: a warning of Judgement, a call to repentance, and a vision of a global harvest. Judgement. Repentance. Harvest. So often we want the Harvest, but we forget that revival is normally preceded by times of national or global crisis (judgement), deep individual and national repentance – and then the outpouring of the Spirit and the harvest of souls.

The Prophet Amos declares: "The lion has roared; who will not fear? The Lord GOD has spoken; who can but prophesy?" (Amos 3:8) He previously proclaimed: "The LORD roars from Zion and raises His voice from Jerusalem; the pastures of the shepherds mourn, and the summit of Carmel withers." (Amos 1:2) In other words, God's voice rings out through the prophetic warnings of judgement and calls to repentance. There is a connection between the true prophetic word and the Fear of the Lord. One of the reasons why there is a lack of the fear of the Lord is because there has been a lack of prophetic proclamation of the One who is to be feared.

The Lion's Roar, is the Lord's roar, he is the Lion of the Tribe of Judah. But the Lion's roar is also heard through the prophets' roar. Are we hearing the Lion's roar? Or are we desperate for things to go back to "business as usual"? Do our online church services have a prophetic edge, or are our church services just simply, "Business as usual?" It's time to awaken the Bride – the King is coming! Before the Lord comes for his church, he desires to come to his church. There will be an international harvest of souls before the Lord's return.

Hosea the prophet states:

> They shall go after the Lord;
> he will roar like a lion;
> when he roars,
> his children shall come trembling from the west;
> they shall come trembling like birds from Egypt,
> and like doves from the land of Assyria,
> and I will return them to their homes, declares the Lord.
>
> (Hosea 11:10-11)

The Lord will bring his lost children home. The lion's roar will cause multitudes to tremble and return to the Lord. For too long the church has purred like a kitten instead of roaring like a lion. The prophetic voice has been a whimper, when it is supposed to resound like thunder. Think about the church at Pentecost. Pentecost was not a pathetic little shower, it was a raging storm! This is why we need revival – revival is nothing less than God restoring the roar. It's time to hear the Lion's roar, and it's time to awaken the prophetic in order that the church might rise up into the fullness of God's purposes in these final hours.

The Lion's Roar

Can you hear the Lion's roar?
It calls the church, once more to soar,
To rise up from the ashes of defeat,
To come before the Mercy Seat,
To leave behind shame and disgrace,
To get on her knees and seek His face.

There is a coming, mighty tide,
The King comes looking for his Bride,
With waves of mercy, waves of grace,
Spot or wrinkle, there can be no trace.
As she gets herself clean, and makes herself holy,
She prepares herself for the coming glory.

And as it was at Pentecost,
The Lord shall usher in the lost,
Tongues of fire – a rushing wind,
Now clothed in white are those who once sinned.

With a sword in their hands, and a fire in their hearts,
Their faith, a shield, from the enemy's darts,
All opposition, they take in their stride,
As God raises up his Warrior Bride.
With consciences cleansed and hearts washed pure,
In a sin-sick world, they bring God's cure.
With banners raised high, they march ahead,

Preaching the gospel and raising the dead.
Awakening sinners, restoring lost sheep,
Those who are slumbering, arise from their sleep.
Cripples are healed, and prisoners set free,
The deaf will hear, the blind will see.

They cast out demons, they speak with new power,
They reflect God's glory, it's the final hour.
They fulfil the commission, empowered from on high,
For this cause, they will live or die.
Their hearts they long, for the return of the King,
As the Day approaches, this new song they sing:

You've opened our eyes, you've broken our chains,
You've healed our hearts, you've washed our stains,
We now lay aside all earthly gain,
You are the Lamb, for us you were slain!

Run with this vision, let hope remain,
The Lord will pour out the latter rain,
Be ever prepared, get into place,
Trust not in yourself, but only his grace.
Know your Lord, yourself, and know your mission;
Keep in your hearts this latter-day vision.
For the time has come, his church to restore,
Listen! Can you hear it? The Lion's Roar!

"'And now,' said Aslan presently, 'to business. I feel I am going to roar. You had better put your fingers in your ears.'"

– *C.S. Lewis, The Lion, the Witch and the Wardrobe.*

If a trumpet is blown in a city will not the people tremble?
If a calamity occurs in a city has not the Lord done it?
Surely the Lord God does nothing
Unless He reveals His secret counsel
To His servants the prophets.
A lion has roared! Who will not fear?
The Lord God has spoken! Who can but prophesy?
Amos 3:6-8
(NASB)

1. The Cry of the Prophets

When the Trumpet blasted in the Old Testament it was time to sit up and take notice. A trumpet blast was a warning blast. It was also a call. A trumpet blast should raise the alarm, only a senseless and complacent people would be indifferent. According to Amos, the prophet's call is likened to the trumpet blast. Further, calamity and disaster is also likened to a trumpet blast and a prophetic wake up call. In other words, when disaster strikes our world, we need to respond as if we were hearing the blast of the trumpet. We need to hear what God is saying prophetically. Do we honestly think that a new virus which is killing many, and which has shut down the global economy, is not a blast of the trumpet? Can we not sense the prophetic nature of the times that we are in?

> If a trumpet is blown in a city will not the people tremble?
> If a calamity occurs in a city has not the Lord done it?
> Surely the Lord God does nothing
> Unless He reveals His secret counsel
> To His servants the prophets.
> A lion has roared! Who will not fear?
> The Lord God has spoken! Who can but prophesy?
> Amos 3:6-8 (NASB)

This passage is one of the most insightful scriptures concerning the role of the prophetic, the sovereignty of God, and the judgements of God.

Amos was a prophet of the Lord who prophesied during the reigns of Uzziah (Judah) and Jeroboam II (Israel). This places Amos' ministry from 792 BC to 753 BC. Amos was called to prophesy to a largely complacent church. Alec Motyer notes the following about the people to whom Amos was prophesying to:

> AFFLUENCE, exploitation, and the profit motive were the most notable features of the society . . .When Amos turned his gaze upon the church he found a religion which was very religious, which adored what was traditional, but which had shaken free from divine revelation. The religious centres were apparently thronged, sacrifices punctiliously offered, the musical side of worship was keenly studied. But it had no basis outside the mind of man. It continued the counterfeit cult of Jeroboam who had set out nearly two centuries earlier to establish a viable alternative to Jerusalem and, with this length of tradition behind it, by the time of Amos it all seemed to be a self-justifying enterprise. The shrines of Jeroboam at Bethel and Dan were still in full operation but under the analytical gaze of Amaze they were but exercises in self-pleasing, abhorrent to God.
>
> The priest, Amaziah, offers us a case history of the best sort of worshipper, but when all came to all, what was he? Establishment-minded, careful for the ecclesiastical proprieties, but supremely disinterested in any word from God.

Wow. Anyone would think that Amos was writing to the western church in the 21st century. Our contemporary churches could easily be described as comfortable, materialistic, happy with traditionalism, excellent worship music, yet ultimately self-serving and resistant to a true Word from the Lord. Equally, Amos' prophetic warning is relevant for us: "The LORD roars from Zion and thunders from Jerusalem; the pastures of the shepherds dry up, and the top of Carmel withers." (Amos 1:2) From the low-land fields, to the mountain tops – this judgement was widespread in its scope. There wasn't any part of the land that wouldn't be affected.

There is clearly a spiritual application here too. The shepherds and the pastures are clearly in view. Like-wise, in the midst of our current pandemic – whilst the nations and the world economies are being shaken, we must recognise that the closure of the houses of worship is part of this shaking too.

However, the nature of the prophetic warning is the subject matter for Chapter Two, our focus here is to highlight the role of the prophetic. God is a God who speaks. He speaks through his prophets, he speaks through his word, he speaks through world events and he speaks through his church. However, when the church becomes like the church in the time of Amos, the prophetic dies out. God's voice becomes lost in the noise of religion. Today, more than ever, we need to rediscover our prophetic calling.

Unlike the Old Testament, where only a few were considered to be prophets, in the New Testament, prophecy is supposed to be the mark of the whole church, and every true Christian.

> And it shall come to pass in the last days, says God,
> That I will pour out of My Spirit on all flesh;
> Your sons and your daughters shall prophesy,
> Your young men shall see visions,
> Your old men shall dream dreams.
> And on My menservants and on My maidservants
> I will pour out My Spirit in those days;
> And they shall prophesy.
> (Acts 2:17-18)

The New Testament, in Eph 4, emphasises the role of prophets, they still have a function in the New Testament era, however, the outpouring of the Spirit upon every believer means that all God's people, to varying degrees, are prophetic.

This is because the prophetic Spirit dwells within every believer. In Revelation 19:10, we read: "For the testimony of Jesus is the spirit of prophecy." In other words, if we have a true testimony in regards to Christ's saving work, that itself is prophetic. There is a work of God being done in you, and it is God's purpose for a work of God to be done through you. You carry within you, as a believer, a prophetic mantle.

You are part of what God is doing in these end times. What is he doing? He is building his church. Not a physical building of brick and stone – a temple of people, filled with the Spirit.

In terms of the "prophetic" there are two major pitfalls and extremes within the church.

At one end of the spectrum, the prophetic is denied. It is assumes that prophecy has "ceased" and that it was only intended for the 'apostolic period'. Those at this end of the spectrum tend to be conservative reformed believers, or traditional evangelicals. Ironically, these are the churches which have a greater emphasis on sola-scriptura – the Bible alone as the final authority for faith and practice. Yet, the Bible itself does not teach that the gifts of the Spirit have ceased, on the contrary the Bible has a lot of instructions about how the New Testament churches should facilitate the gift of prophecy. The point at which cessationists deny the gift of prophecy, is precisely the point where they cease to hold to sola-scriptura. It is at this point they exalt human tradition above the Word of God. The Word of God is crystal clear when it comes to the on-going function of prophecy, it is the tradition of man that muddies the waters.

Leaders in the cessationist camp are in real danger of grieving the Holy Spirit. They have raised up congregations that are stone deaf to the Spirit. This is a serious sin and must be repented of.

At the other end of the spectrum, particularly at the extreme end of the charismatic movement – many leaders and Christians have prostituted the prophetic. The awe-inspiring word of the Lord has been traded for an ear-tickling, ego-boosting fortune cookie. These prophets are like the false prophets in Jeremiah's time, they prophesy 'peace, peace' when there is no peace. They are too busy building a platform for their own glory that they are blind to the true Word of the Lord. This current shake up is a judgement on many false ministries. The following example from Jeremiah Johnson was posted on the 9th April, and it's a sobering warning to the false prophetic ministries.

> One of the number one questions I am being asked by saints around the body of Christ right now is why are so many "apostles" and "prophets" quiet in the midst of COVID-19. A phone call I received yesterday might give us some insight.
>
> His voice was shaky and he was crying. A well-known minister called me yesterday. I said, "What's wrong brother?". He replied, "COVID-19 has shut down my ministry." I said, "Well yes brother there isn't much traveling and public speaking going on right now." He shouted back, "No! You don't understand Jeremiah. I have realised during this pandemic that the message and gospel that I have been preaching is not the real gospel.
>
> It doesn't work in the midst of suffering. I cannot promise blessing and prosperity to anyone.

All the free upgrades, promotions, and messages that are centered upon people is not the real gospel and I was totally blind to it!"

I was silent on the other end of the phone. Dumbfounded actually. Primarily because this man is recognised in many circles as a well known apostle and prophet. Hundreds gather at his meetings for their blessing and next upgrade. He broke my silence with a prophetic warning that I did not expect. "Jeremiah," he said, "Watch in the next 30-60 days. Many of the apostles and prophets who have had no true word of the Lord during this crisis will resume back to their old tactics and tricks. They will go back to a me-centered gospel and get the people hollering again. The seed offerings and gimmicks are going to explode."

I thanked him for his honesty and we prayed together. True repentance took place. I also experienced the fear of the Lord in a profound way.

Could some apostles and prophets be silent right now because they are resting and recharging in a healthy way? Yes! Could this bombshell confession and prophetic warning from this well-known minister be the truth as well? You better believe it!

Many have sounded the alarm at the abuses that have been taking place in the prophetic movement for years. Sadly these abuses have caused many sincere believers to neglect or reject the gift of prophecy all together. I have to confess that excess and abuse of prophecy is one of the factors that caused me to move towards more conservative church circles.

The result being that I didn't emphasise the importance of the gifts of the Spirit for almost seven years. However, the Lord made it very plain to me that a ministry or denomination that rejects the present day working of the Holy Spirit is at risk of being a ministry of the flesh. It may not look as fleshly as the extreme end of the charismatic movement, but hidden beneath a veneer of respectability there can exist a world of fleshly control, human pride, and hidden sin. Sin is very comfortable and hides in plain sight when we shut down the prophetic voice. The prophetic voice is needed to keep us transparent and accountable.

The problem is not that God is not speaking; the problem is that we have become deaf to his voice. We have become insensitive to his heartbeat. We have reduced preaching to a talk or a lecture when God's purpose was for the preacher to bring burning coals from the altar. At best our sermons are faint echoes of the Word of God. Preaching is supposed to be prophetic. It is supposed to be a NOW word from the Lord. Even now, in the midst of our pandemic, when church services have gone online, very little has changed with our preaching. Our shift from church buildings to online services feels a bit like rearranging the chairs on the Titanic whilst the ship is sinking. We are in a spiritual wilderness and we need John the Baptist-like voices to prepare the way of the Lord.

Like John the Baptist, and many other prophetic types, the Lord has been preparing many believers for these times. The recent pandemic has blind-sided many pastors, leaders and Christians, but this is not the case for everyone. A number of God's people have been in the furnace of God's preparation for 'such a time as this.' Whilst many churches have come to rest on the wisdom and ways of man to develop their brand, and build a 'successful ministry', the Lord has been working in the lives of many 'Davids' who have been overlooked and relegated to the fields. The time has come for many of God's overlooked and rejected ones to rise up into their calling.

Many of God's chosen vessels have sat on the sidelines whist the church pursues innovation after innovation. They have endured watered down gospel preaching for decades. They have noticed the shift from preaching about holiness, to well-being. They can count on one hand how many sermons they have heard that unpack the Bible's teaching on sin, judgement, hell and repentance. Deep down they know the church has become increasingly comfortable with a lukewarm message delivered to lukewarm people with lukewarm words.

Many of God's Kingdom-people have become neutered because they are shackled to churches which are building empires of men instead of the kingdom of God. Cronyism is rife amongst denominational leaders.

Many leaders at the top of the denominational chain get there the same way that people in secular business get there – they become company men, rather than kingdom men. There is no room for the prophet. The prophetic anointing is the antithesis of the institutional structure.

Many in our churches have been branded "troublemakers" and "divisive" because they dared to question the status quo, or even challenge injustice or a lack of integrity amongst leaders. In an amazing sleight of the hand, such leaders turn on these "whistle-blowers" and condemn them.

A number of non-Christians have more insight than the church in these days. They recognise that there are many toxic elements to our 21st century lives. Many are rejoicing at the opportunity to spend more time with their family, or to see the skies clear of pollution, or even to be given some respite from all the chaos of modern life. Sadly, many in the church are blind to the toxic elements of our church cultures – so they are exporting them online, and they are desperate to get back to 'business as usual'.

But what if God does not want us to get back to business as usual? What if this shake up is a call for us to drop everything that is non-essential in our church life? What if this is a call to discover the basic elements of New Testament Christianity? What if God actually wants our denominations to die? What if that building project was never his idea in the first place?

Maybe he wants the church to go back to meeting in homes, rather than temples? Maybe it's time for many who are 'full-time' to discover a tent-making ministry, so that the local body of believers be released into their ministry? The work of the church was never supposed to be predominantly the work of one or two paid staff members. Is God stripping our empires back to bare essentials?

I don't claim to perceive all that God is saying or doing in these times. Far from it. However, what seems clear is the fact that the lion is roaring, and the trumpet is being sounded. This means we are being called to examine ourselves. We are being called to deep heart-searching, and deep repentance. As individuals, we must deal with our personal and secret sins – lust, temper, dishonesty, manipulation etc. most of which are driven by deep rooted fears. – it's time to get set free from things that have held us back for years. At a church level: it's time to repent of our ecclesiastical sins – pride, arrogance, love of power, spiritual abuse, religiosity, empire building, indifference to the lost, prayerlessness, etc. At a national, and international level, there needs to be *en masse* personal repentance for forsaking the Lord and his moral standards. We're slaughtering infants in the womb, destroying the family unit, confusing young people about gender, and evicting God from public life. We have created a godless society and we are reaping what we have sown. It's time to return to the Lord because his return is at hand.

When I shut up the heavens so that there is no rain, or command the locust to devour the land, or send pestilence among my people, if my people who are called by my name humble themselves, and pray and seek my face and turn from their wicked ways, then I will hear from heaven and will forgive their sin and heal their land.

(2 Chron. 7:13-14)

"They say Aslan is on the move- perhaps has already landed." And now a very curious thing happened. None of the children knew who Aslan was any more than you do; but the moment the Beaver had spoken these words everyone felt quite different. Perhaps it has sometimes happened to you in a dream that someone says something which you don't understand but in the dream it feels as if it has some enormous meaning- either a terrifying one which turns the whole dream into a nightmare or else a lovely meaning too lovely to put into words, which makes the dream so beautiful that you remember it all your life and are always wishing you could get into that dream again. It was like that now."

C.S. Lewis, The Lion, the Witch and the Wardrobe

2. A Warning of Judgement

It's impossible to read the Old Testament prophets, and not see the theme of God's Judgement. Like-wise, it's impossible to look closely at the ministry of John the Baptist, Jesus, and the Apostles, and not see the theme of God's judgement. Those who claim that the Old Testament reveals God's judgement, and the New Testament reveals his grace, have clearly not studied either with any degree of care. Grace and judgement are both factors of both Old and New Testaments.

Yet when we look at much of the contemporary church we see a clear pattern: Firstly, very few prophets prophesy anything about sin, judgement or repentance (in fact many prophetic schools actively forbid these kinds of prophecies);

Secondly, very few Bible Teachers or gospel preachers preach on sin, judgement and repentance; thirdly, very few Christians are willing to interpret natural disasters as being either "from God" or "allowed by God" or even "used by God". Hardly any Christian is willing to claim that the Coronavirus, and its wider effects are a judgement from God. In fact, most Christians I've encountered actively oppose that view.

Yet, this is not what our prophet Amos teaches us. Let us return to the scripture we were reflecting on in the previous chapter.

If a trumpet is blown in a city will not the people

tremble?
If a calamity occurs in a city has not the LORD done it?
Surely the Lord GOD does nothing
Unless He reveals His secret counsel
To His servants the prophets.
A lion has roared! Who will not fear?
The Lord GOD has spoken! Who can but prophesy?
Amos 3:6-8 (NASB)

This series of rhetorical questions is designed to make a point. If the trumpet blows – yes, the people should tremble. If calamity strikes a city – yes, the Lord has done it. If Coronavirus strikes the nations and brings the economy grinding to a halt, has not the Lord done it? Of course he has. The Lord is sovereign. He is not the author of evil, but the Bible clearly reveals that God allows calamities, the devil, and even the evil actions of people to bring about his purposes.

In contrast to the prevailing views in the modern church, I am absolutely convinced that the Coronavirus pandemic is a wakeup call from God. It's a trumpet blast. It is the roar of the Lion. John Piper puts it this way: "The coronavirus is God's thunderclap call for all of us to repent and realign our lives with the infinite worth of Christ." Yet despite the thundering many believers remain oblivious to heaven's wakeup call.

David Wilkerson, in his book 'The Vision and Beyond' prophesied and predicted a number of judgements that would shake the world. He predicted economic collapse and a series of natural disasters including earthquakes, wars and plagues. On a few occasions he uses the phrase "nature's revenge". Interestingly, in the last couple of weeks, I've heard atheists use the same phrase. One atheist saw the virus as a kickback for the gross injustice that humanity is acting out against both the environment and the animal kingdom. Another atheist saw it as nature's cull. In some respects both of these atheists are more morally alert than many in the church who think what is happening has no correlation to the moral actions of humanity. Here is how Wilkerson says believers are to interpret 'nature's revenge'.

Discerning people will have within them an innate knowledge that God is behind these strange events and is unleashing the fury of nature to force men into a mood of concern about eternal values. These violent reactions of nature will be clearly orchestrated by God to warn mankind of the coming days of wrath and judgement. It is almost as though all heaven is crying out, "Oh Earth, heed his call. He holds the pillars of Earth in his hands. He will shake the earth until his voice is heard. He rides King of the Flood and Lord of the Winds and Rains.[1]

---

[1] Wilkerson, David, The Vision, p32.

If discerning people understand that these events are orchestrated by God, our contemporary church must be in a terrible state. Where is the church's discernment when God can shake the nations and Christian believers can settle into their lockdowns with no sense of conviction of sin, no sense of looming judgement, and no sense of the call to deep prayer and repentance?

Why do we no longer see God as a God of Judgement? Part of the issue, I think, is the fact that we have misunderstood the nature of God. We have been spoon fed sermonettes about God's grace, love, and goodness to the point where we have lost all sense of the majesty, greatness and glory of God. Have we lost sight of the fact that God is all-powerful and holy? He is a God of justice.

As a result of this, too many people polarise God's judgement and his grace, and his love and his wrath, as if they were completely unconnected. The reality is, God's judgement is as much a manifestation of his love as his grace is. Judgement is an act of love. Think about it in the natural, if we did not have courts, judges, and prisons we would have a very cruel society. As a society, we expect justice when people break the law. Justice is an essential foundation for the well-being of society. God's judgements are no different, they are an act of love designed to bring sinful humanity back into alignment with his will. God's judgements are a manifestation of his mercy.

The psalmist put it this way, "Before I was afflicted I went astray, but now I keep your word." (Psalm 119:67) In other words, God's judgement and discipline brought affliction upon the psalmist as he turned astray from God, as a result, the psalmist turned to God in his affliction. This is the gospel. This is the story of the prodigal son. It's reflected in many of our hymns, not least Amazing Grace. How we have ever lost sight of this foundational truth is a mystery. Yet our departure from truth does not change the reality of it one bit. God remains the same.

A.W. Tozer also speaks about the goodness of God's judgement. Tozer says,

> Since God's first concern for His universe is its moral health, that is, its holiness, whatever is contrary to this is necessarily under His eternal displeasure. To preserve His creation God must destroy whatever would destroy it.
>
> When He arises to put down iniquity and save the world from irreparable moral collapse, He is said to be angry. Every wrathful judgment in the history of the world has been a holy act of preservation. The holiness of God, the wrath of God, and the health of the creation are inseparably united. God's wrath is His utter intolerance of whatever degrades and destroys. He hates iniquity as a mother hates the polio that takes the life of her child.[2]

---

[2] Tozer, A.W., Knowledge of the Holy.

We mustn't lose sight of the fact that God is loving, holy, and just, and because he is all of these things he acts in judgement and wrath. We make a mistake if we think that "judgement" always means "condemnation". Whilst God's judgement does manifest in condemnation, we need to remember that God sends judgements in order to lead us to repentance. Pharaoh could have saved himself a lot of pain and heartache had he not continually hardened his heart. Had he released God's people from slavery, he could have avoided judgement. Even when the judgements started, he could have repented, but instead he hardened his heart to the point of no return. When we do this, we are setting ourselves up for eternal condemnation. We have chosen God's wrath rather than his mercy.

We see this principle time and time again throughout scripture. In Luke's gospel, Jesus gives the following account:

> There were some present at that very time who told him about the Galileans whose blood Pilate had mingled with their sacrifices. And he answered them, "Do you think that these Galileans were worse sinners than all the other Galileans, because they suffered in this way?
>
> No, I tell you; but unless you repent, you will all likewise perish. Or those eighteen on whom the tower in Siloam fell and killed them: do you think that they were worse offenders than all the others who lived in Jerusalem? No, I tell you; but unless you repent, you will all likewise perish.

(Luke 13:1-5)

This passage is very relevant, firstly because it covers all kinds of suffering – both moral and natural. Pilate slaughtered some worshippers (moral) and a tower fell on some victims (natural). Jesus makes it clear that those who died were not worse sinners than others who were alive at the time. This is important. When we say that the Coronavirus is a judgement from God, we are not saying that God is specifically taking aim at those who are infected and get ill, or even die. No. But as a societal judgement, whenever calamity strikes there is a warning for all of us. What is the warning? Time is short. Life is fragile and uncertain. We must be ready because we do not know the day or the hour when we will breathe our last. We must recognise our need to repent, and we must get ourselves right with God. When judgement strikes the land, it is a warning.

Some of the severest judgements we read about in scripture are found in the book of Revelation. John writes:

> When he opened the sixth seal, I looked, and behold, there was a great earthquake, and the sun became black as sackcloth, the full moon became like blood, and the stars of the sky fell to the earth as the fig tree sheds its winter fruit when shaken by a gale. The sky vanished like a scroll that is being rolled up, and every mountain and island was removed from its place.

> Then the kings of the earth and the great ones and the generals and the rich and the powerful, and everyone, slave and free, hid themselves in the caves and among the rocks of the mountains, calling to the mountains and rocks, "Fall on us and hide us from the face of him who is seated on the throne, and from the wrath of the Lamb, for the great day of their wrath has come, and who can stand?"
>
> (Rev. 6:12-17)

These judgements are so severe they make the Coronavirus look like a walk in in the park. Yet this passage reveals the haunting reality that there are various degrees of God's judgements. Judgements vary in their severity. Some seem minor, and others seem major. Further, every earthly judgement is child's play in contrast to the final judgement – eternal wrath and condemnation. Yet one of the reasons that God sends temporal judgements is to bring us to repentance so that we may never have to experience eternal judgement. Yet this passage in Revelation shows us the true nature of humanity – we would rather be crushed by mountains and rocks than bow the knee to the Lord Jesus Christ. We are no different to Pharaoh, despite judgements and warnings; we would rather cling stubbornly to our self-will than repent and turn to God.

We must never lose sight of God's purpose in sending warnings and temporal judgements – God's heart is for us to return to him – his desire is that we discover the gift of repentance.

And the Lord has sent to you all His servants the prophets again and again, but you have not listened nor inclined your ear to hear, saying, 'Turn now everyone from his evil way and from the evil of your deeds, and dwell on the land which the Lord has given to you and your forefathers forever and ever; and do not go after other gods to serve them and to worship them, and do not provoke Me to anger with the work of your hands, and I will do you no harm.' (Jer, 25:4-6)

Not only does a lion's roar mark out the boundaries of its territory, but it can also be a rallying point for straying members of its tribe. This has amazing prophetic implications as we enter a season of a harvest of souls and a transition from priestly ministry into kingly ministry. Perhaps this roar of the Lion King is signifying great change is coming!

Dr. James W. Goll

3. A Call to Repentance

There is a heaven to be gained and a hell to be shunned. That is Biblical truth. Jesus said it plainly; there are two roads – a narrow road, and a broad road. The broad road leads to hell and destruction, and the narrow road leads to life. Because of Adam's fall, and our own sins, every single one of us is born on the road to destruction. No one is heaven bound by nature, and no one is heaven bound because they are a good person. The only way to get off the broad road and on to the narrow road is by repenting. We need to repent. There is a future day of judgement, and we are headed for condemnation, unless we repent.

Are these ideas not old-fashioned? Is this not the religion of less educated times? Surely such thinking belongs to another era – it belongs to a pre-enlightenment age? Let me suggest that there has never been a time when the message of repentance was considered contemporary. By and large it has always led people to mock. I'm sure Noah was mocked as insane – right up until the flood came and the door of the ark was closed. The true prophets in the Old Testament were often disregarded because their message was regarded as too doom and gloom.

Let's look at some examples of God's call to repentance in the scriptures. Mark's Gospel kicks off with a vivid description of John the Baptist's ministry.

> John appeared, baptizing in the wilderness and proclaiming a baptism of repentance for the forgiveness of sins. And all the country of Judea and all Jerusalem were going out to him and were being baptized by him in the river Jordan, confessing their sins.
>
> (Mark 1:4-5)

This was a move of the Spirit of God. Only God can cause the crowds to respond positively to a message of Judgement and repentance. Of course, John's message was a message of grace too – the baptism pointed forward to the cleansing and grace that would come through Jesus Christ. It's not one or the other. Repentance and grace belong in the same message. Repentance is grace, and grace is repentance. We need to stop thinking in polarised ways.

Sadly the church has often been divided by traditional, harsh legalists at one end of the spectrum, and cheap-grace, sugar-coated gospel preachers at the other end. Both are a distortion of the true biblical gospel. The gospel is both judgement and mercy, and grace and repentance. God is love, and he is holy – his love is a holy love. We must recover the full gospel in these days that we are living in. We must preach the terrifying realities of hell – but we must do so with tears in our eyes and love in our hearts. Remember, it was God the Son who tasted hell for us. God the Son absorbed the wrath of a righteous God in order that hell-deserving sinners like you and me could be forgiven and saved.

Admittedly, proclaiming the judgement to come and the call to repentance is not easy. There is a stigma attached – this is one of the reasons we need to make sure we are moving in the fullness and the power of the Holy Spirit. The anointing is no guarantee that you won't look stupid, but at the very least your message will carry power. If you hope to stand against a tide of ridicule, mockery and opposition, you don't want to be standing in your own strength. Your own flesh will make you look even more foolish. Any message of judgement and repentance should be birthed out of prayer, intercession and time in God's presence – the stronger the message, the greater the need for fasting and prayer. When we begin to preach repentance and judgement, we are moving into frontline spiritual warfare – and we can only do that clothed with power and authority from on high. And yet – even with divine commission and empowering, there is no guarantee that our message will produce the results that we want to see – even Paul experienced ridicule.

> "Therefore since we are God's offspring, we should not think that the divine being is like gold or silver or stone—an image made by human design and skill. In the past God overlooked such ignorance, but now he commands all people everywhere to repent. For he has set a day when he will judge the world with justice by the man he has appointed. He has given proof of this to everyone by raising him from the dead."

> When they heard about the resurrection of the dead, some of them sneered, but others said, "We want to hear you again on this subject." At that, Paul left the Council. Some of the people became followers of Paul and believed. Among them was Dionysius, a member of the Areopagus, also a woman named Damaris, and a number of others.
>
> (Acts 17:29-34)

This is what apostolic preaching looks like. Notice the lack of positive confession, self-esteem and pseudo-psychology. Paul, having laid the foundation of the nature of God and creation, gets straight to the heart of the issue – their idolatry. He identifies their sin, and calls them to repent. Just like Jesus did. Just like John the Baptist did. And just like the prophets did.

Next let's look at the response – some sneered, and others wanted to book him for another slot – that wasn't sincere follow up, it's just because they enjoyed listening to speakers – they wanted entertainment. Paul was having none of it. His job was done. He left. However – he did reap a small harvest. Never underestimate the effectiveness of the Word of God when it is preached faithfully.

In many ways our churches in the west are in a very similar situation to that which the Hebrew believers were in. Let's have a look at Hebrews for a moment.

> About this we have much to say, and it is hard to explain, since you have become dull of hearing. For though by this time you ought to be teachers, you need someone to teach you again the basic principles of the oracles of God. You need milk, not solid food, for everyone who lives on milk is unskilled in the word of righteousness, since he is a child. But solid food is for the mature, for those who have their powers of discernment trained by constant practice to distinguish good from evil.
>
> (Heb 5:11-14)
>
> Therefore let us leave the elementary doctrine of Christ and go on to maturity, not laying again a foundation of repentance from dead works and of faith toward God, and of instruction about washings, the laying on of hands, the resurrection of the dead, and eternal judgment.
>
> (Heb. 6:1-2)

Firstly, the writer (we don't know who wrote Hebrews) challenges the believers in terms of their spiritual maturity. Notice the frankness with which the writer speaks – he calls them dull of hearing, babies who are still sucking their mother's breast, and unequipped for ministry. If a leader spoke to us like that today we'd go running to our safe-space for a month. We'd want the leader hauled over the coals for spiritual abuse.

Yet this is the Holy Spirit speaking. The Holy Spirit is very non-British. Despite the urban myth, he is anything but a gentleman! The Holy Spirit is a straight talker who doesn't pull his punches – there is nothing gentleman-like about that.

The next thing the writer does is remind the believers what the foundational, elementary, basic teachings of the church are – and repentance is amongst them. Again, the believers are being rebuked – by this stage they should be mature, and able to instruct others, the reality is they need to go back to primary school and re-learn their ABC's!

Are we any different? Eternal judgement and repentance are regarded as foundational doctrines yet they are all but missing from our western spiritual vocabulary. The reality is the western church is trapped in infancy. We are like that adult that we've met – the one who has never grown up, taken responsibility, or been corrected – the kind who throws a tantrum when he doesn't get his own way. That's the western church – we have a deeply entrenched sense of entitlement and arrogance, but the reality is we are spiritual babies.

We need to learn from the new believers in China and Brazil – they will demonstrate their grasp of repentance and the judgement to come – and their message will be backed up with signs, wonders and miracles!

Repentance is foundational to both the gospel message, and Christian discipleship. Repentance and baptism is the gateway into the kingdom of God, but repentance is also on-going. Repentance is not a one-off event. As we seek to become more Christ-like, we should be sensitive to the Spirit's conviction – he will lead us to repent of inner-heart attitudes such as pride, anger, lust, or forgiveness. On-going repentance is the key to spiritual growth.

We see some very powerful examples of repentance in the life of believers in the Bible. David is a classic. Let's take a moment to look at David's repentance.

We know the story. He lusted after Bathsheba, he then acted on his lust and had sex with her, and he then tried to cover this up by getting her husband drunk so the husband would think it was him who got his wife pregnant. When this failed, David set the husband up to be killed at war. David then hides his sin, and carries on with "business as usual". David is in a classic backslidden state – yet he is still in office. He is still carrying on with his ministry. It takes an encounter with a prophet (Nathan) who said to David, ("You are the man!") before David is convicted and comes to repentance: ("I have sinned against the Lord.")

What does repentance look like? David again is helpful here – his repentance is recorded for all to see in Psalm 51. We too can use Psalm 51 as a framework for our own prayer of repentance. Before you read the next section, make sure you have 15-30 minutes of uninterrupted time so you can prayerfully mediate on the following Psalm. Use this Psalm to take ownership of your sins. Ask the Holy Spirit to reveal certain sins that you need to bring to the blood. The good news is, we don't need the blood of animal sacrifices because we have the blood of Jesus Christ. As he brings specific sins to mind, pray this: *Lord, I renounce _____ in Jesus' name, forgive me and wash me in your blood.*

Psalm 51

Have mercy on me, O God,
    according to your steadfast love;
according to your abundant mercy
    blot out my transgressions.
[2] Wash me thoroughly from my iniquity,
    and cleanse me from my sin!
[3] For I know my transgressions,
    and my sin is ever before me.
[4] Against you, you only, have I sinned
    and done what is evil in your sight,
so that you may be justified in your words
    and blameless in your judgment.

⁵ Behold, I was brought forth in iniquity,
    and in sin did my mother conceive me.
⁶ Behold, you delight in truth in the inward being,
    and you teach me wisdom in the secret heart.
        ⁷ Purge me with hyssop, and I shall be clean;
    wash me, and I shall be whiter than snow.
⁸ Let me hear joy and gladness;
    let the bones that you have broken rejoice.
⁹ Hide your face from my sins,
    and blot out all my iniquities.
¹⁰ Create in me a clean heart, O God,
    and renew a right spirit within me.
¹¹ Cast me not away from your presence,
    and take not your Holy Spirit from me.

¹² Restore to me the joy of your salvation,
    and uphold me with a willing spirit.
        ¹³ Then I will teach transgressors your ways,
    and sinners will return to you.
¹⁴ Deliver me from bloodguiltiness, O God,
    O God of my salvation,
    and my tongue will sing aloud of your righteousness.
¹⁵ O Lord, open my lips,
    and my mouth will declare your praise.
¹⁶ For you will not delight in sacrifice, or I would give it;
    you will not be pleased with a burnt offering.
¹⁷ The sacrifices of God are a broken spirit;
    a broken and contrite heart, O God, you will not despise.

> [18] Do good to Zion in your good pleasure;
> build up the walls of Jerusalem;
> [19] then will you delight in right sacrifices,
> in burnt offerings and whole burnt offerings;
> then bulls will be offered on your altar.

Once you have prayed through this, thank God for the blood of Jesus Christ. The blood of Jesus is sufficient to cleanse us perfectly. There is no sin that is bigger than the blood of Jesus Christ.

> But if we walk in the light, as he is in the light, we have fellowship with one another, and the blood of Jesus his Son cleanses us from all sin. If we say we have no sin, we deceive ourselves, and the truth is not in us.
>
> If we confess our sins, he is faithful and just to forgive us our sins and to cleanse us from all unrighteousness. If we say we have not sinned, we make him a liar, and his word is not in us.
>
> (1 John 1:7-10)

Now that you have confessed and renounced your sins, and brought them to the cross, ask God the Father fill you with His Holy Spirit. Raise your hands, and worship and thank him – the river of God will begin to flow through your Spirit as you do.

I am roaring out of Zion. I am coming as an Eagle to My temple. I am coming to judge and make war. I am coming to tear down the walls of untempered mortar. The walls of division and strife. I am making war against the spirit of slavery and oppression. I am judging between the sheep and the goats. The wheat and the chaff. I am laying the axe of My will to the root of the trees. I will separate says the Lord. I will divide and I will judge. I will make a righteous judgment over the land.

Prophetic Word by Chad Taylor

4. The Fear of the Lord

No Fear is a sports brand that was incredibly popular amongst boxers in the 1990s. As a young amateur boxer, two of my proudest possessions were my No Fear hats. No Fear captures the warrior spirit. No Fear is the sign of a champion. No Fear could also be the slogan for the church in the west – but not in a good way. RT Kendall says, "It is my opinion that the greatest absence in the church today is the fear of God."[3] In other words – when it comes to God, there is no fear.

RT Kendall, in his book, 'Whatever Happened to the Gospel?' connects the loss of the fear of the Lord with the subject of our previous chapter – the loss of emphasis on judgement and repentance. Kendall states:

> Have you ever thought about the absence of preaching and teaching on Hell and eternal punishment? Have you become concerned about the lack of the fear of God in church and society? Have you wondered if there might be a correlation between the absence of the fear of God and the absence of belief in eternal punishment?[4]

The answer to each of these rhetorical questions should be yes!

---

[3] R.T. Kendall, Holy Fire: A Balanced, Biblical Look at the Holy Spirit's Work in Our Lives

[4] R.T. Kendall, Whatever Happened to the Gospel?

Yes there is an absence of preaching on these topics, yes we should be concerned at the lack of the fear of the Lord in church and society, and yes there is a connection between the loss of the fear of the Lord and the lack of belief about hell.

Let me ask you a question. Do you just 'believe' in hell because you are a 'Bible Christian' and you kind of have too because it's in the book? Do you treat it like an unpleasant part of a contract – it's there, but you don't think about it too much and it's not considered the most relevant topic? Whilst we would never admit it, I think that is exactly how many Bible-believing Christians approach the topic of hell.

Let me ask you another question – have you ever *felt* the Bible's teaching on hell? This is a work of the Spirit. The apostle John says: "And when he comes, he will convict the world concerning sin and righteousness and judgment." (John 16:8) In other words, the Holy Spirit will impress upon the person a deep subconscious sense of divine judgement.

We can experience this at various levels. It is this work of the Spirit that leads a person to repentance: the deeper the conviction, the deeper the repentance. However, the shallower the preaching, the less conviction there is, and the less repentance there will be. Or to put it the another way, the stronger the preaching, the stronger the conviction, the deeper the repentance will be.

We see this illustrated in many of the past revivals.

Jonathan Edwards is one example this kind of preaching. His sermon, 'Sinners in the hands of an Angry God' is a powerful example. Before we look at the effects of that sermon, let us look at some of the content. Edwards was preaching on Deuteronomy 32:35, "Their foot shall slide in due time." Read the following extract, carefully and prayerfully.

> You probably are not sensible of this; you find you are kept out of hell, but do not see the hand of God in it; but look at other things, as the good state of your bodily constitution, your care of your own life, and the means you use for your own preservation.
>
> But indeed these things are nothing; if God should withdraw his hand, they would avail no more to keep you from falling, than the thin air to hold up a person that is suspended in it.
>
> Your wickedness makes you as it were heavy as lead, and to tend downwards with great weight and pressure towards hell; and if God should let you go, you would immediately sink and swiftly descend and plunge into the bottomless gulf, and your healthy constitution, and your own care and prudence, and best contrivance, and all your righteousness, would have no more influence to uphold you and keep you out of hell, than a spider's web would have to stop a fallen rock.
>
> Were it not for the sovereign pleasure of God, the earth would not bear you one moment; for you are a burden to it.

> The creation groans with you; the creature is made subject to the bondage of your corruption, not willingly; the sun does not willingly shine upon you to give you light to serve sin and Satan; the earth does not willingly yield her increase to satisfy your lusts; nor is it willingly a stage for your wickedness to be acted upon; the air does not willingly serve you for breath to maintain the flame of life in your vitals, while you spend your life in the service of God's enemies.

I'm confident that most contemporary believers would react negatively to Edward's sermon: 'Sinners in the Hands of an Angry God.' I'm sure almost none of us will have sat under a sermon anywhere near as graphic or challenging as that. Most of us would recoil at such a message. Yet this message was preached in the midst of revival. And dare I say it – this kind preaching is the preaching of revival – revival is extreme – and so is revival preaching. I think some of us only want the thrills of revival – we don't really want the extremities of revival. Regarding the effects of Edward's historic sermon one commentator notes:

> Sinners in the hand of an angry God was a powerful sermon preached by Jonathan Edwards at Enfield, Connecticut on July 8, 1741, during the American Revival known as "the Great Awakening." His sermon was interrupted many times by people moaning and crying out "What shall I do to be saved?"[5]

---

[5] http://bibletruthchatroom.com/2012/06/preaching-with-tears/

In other words, deep conviction of sin broke upon the crowds who gathered to listen. Don't misunderstand me – this is not something that can be manufactured – there is a certain kind of conservative preacher and church who try to manufacture this kind of thing – and it's dead.

Many of the old school Scottish Presbyterian churches that you will find scattered throughout the highlands and islands are of this kind of variety. So are some fundamentalist Baptists. But this is not some kind of legalistic, false reverence we are describing here – this is the blazing anointing of the Holy Spirit pouring forth from a preacher who has been broken before the Lord. Many preachers should never dare to preach like this until they have wept for days under a deep conviction for their own sins and the souls of the lost.

In fact, this baptism of power (which we will look at in more detail in a later chapter) is the essential qualification for this kind of ministry. Preaching hell and judgement alone is not enough – in fact, preaching hell and judgement with divine empowerment is dangerous. When a person is empowered from on high, they don't need to preach as graphically as Edwards to produce this kind of conviction – preaching the grace of Christ can equally pierce the hearts of the listeners. Charles Finney writes about his experience in this area.

> This power is a great marvel. I have many times seen people unable to endure the word.

The most simple and ordinary statements would cut men off from their seats like a sword, would take away their bodily strength, and render them almost as helpless as dead men. Several times it has been true in my experience that I could not raise my voice, or say anything in prayer or exhortation except in the mildest manner, without wholly overcoming those that were present. This was not because I was preaching terror to the people; but the sweetest sounds of the gospel would overcome them.

This power seems sometimes to pervade the atmosphere of one who is highly charged with it. Many times great numbers of persons in a community will be clothed with this power, when the very atmosphere of the whole place seems to be charged with the life of God. Strangers coming into it, and passing through the place, will be instantly smitten with conviction of sin, and in many instances converted to Christ. When Christians humble themselves, and consecrate their all afresh to Christ, and ask for this power, they will often receive such a baptism that they will be instrumental in converting more souls in one day than in all their lifetime before. While Christians remain humble enough to retain this power the work of conversion will go on, till whole communities and regions of country are converted to Christ. The same is true of ministers.[6]

Here is another account from Finney:

---

[6] Charles Finney, Power from on High.

In a few moments there seemed to fall upon the congregation an instantaneous shock. I cannot describe the sensation that I felt, nor that which was apparent in the congregation; but the word seemed literally to cut like a sword. The power from on high came down upon them in such a torrent that they fell from their seats in every direction. In less than a minute nearly the whole congregation were either down on their knees, or on their faces, or in some position prostrate before God.

Everyone was crying or groaning for mercy upon his own soul. They paid no further attention to me or to my preaching. I tried to get their attention; but I could not. I observed the aged man who had invited me there as still retaining his seat near the centre of the house. He was staring around him with a look of unutterable astonishment. Pointing to him, I cried at the top of my voice, "Can't you pray?" He knelt down and roared out a short prayer, about as loud as he could holler, but they paid no attention to him.

After looking round for a few moments, I knelt down and put my hand on the head of a young man who was kneeling at my feet, and engaged in prayer for mercy on his soul. I got his attention, and preached Jesus in his ear. In a few moments he seized Jesus by faith, and then broke out in prayer for those around him. I then turned to another in the same way, and with the same result; and then another, and another, till I know not how many had laid hold of Christ and were full of prayer for others.[7]

---

[7] Finney, Power.

Countless further examples could be given to demonstrate the Spirit's work of convicting people of their sins and bringing them to repentance. Any serious study of revival will reveal that this is an essential feature of any genuine revival. This is not to suggest that ecstatic joy is not also a mark of revival, but the normal order is conviction followed by repentance which in turn is followed by high praise and overflowing joy. The Lord must strike us before he heals us. Before he can build us up, he must tear us down in order to make sure we are building on a true foundation of humility and repentance.

It's one thing to look at examples from revivals of the past, but what about the Bible? The Bible from Genesis to Revelation is full of references to the fear of the Lord. Like repentance, it is a foundational issue. If we have no experience of the fear of the Lord, we really have no experience of the Lord.

Here are some scriptures which demonstrate the importance of the fear of the Lord:

The fear of the Lord is the beginning of knowledge; fools despise wisdom and instruction. (Prov. 1:7)

The fear of the Lord is hatred of evil. Pride and arrogance and the way of evil and perverted speech I hate. (Prov. 8:13)

Let all the earth fear the Lord; let all the inhabitants of the world stand in awe of him! (Psalm 33:8)

> The friendship of the Lord is for those who fear him, and he makes known to them his covenant. (Psalm 25:14)
>
> And now, Israel, what does the Lord your God require of you, but to fear the Lord your God, to walk in all his ways, to love him, to serve the Lord your God with all your heart and with all your soul. (Deut. 10:12)
>
> Since we have these promises, beloved, let us cleanse ourselves from every defilement of body and spirit, bringing holiness to completion in the fear of God. (2 Cor. 7:1)
>
> Honour everyone. Love the brotherhood. Fear God. Honour the emperor. (1 Pet. 2:17)
>
> So the church throughout all Judea and Galilee and Samaria had peace and was being built up. And walking in the fear of the Lord and in the comfort of the Holy Spirit, it multiplied. (Acts 9:31)
>
> And if you call on him as Father who judges impartially according to each one's deeds, conduct yourselves with fear throughout the time of your exile, (1 Peter 1:17)
>
> Submitting to one another out of reverence for Christ. (Eph. 5:21)
>
> Therefore, knowing the fear of the Lord, we persuade others. But what we are is known to God, and I hope it is known also to your conscience. (2 Cor. 5:11)

These scriptures are just the tip of the iceberg, there are many more, but hopefully they are a fresh reminder for us to see that the fear of the Lord is an essential thread that runs through both the Old and New Testaments.

Of course, it is also true that the Bible is full of examples where we are instructed not to fear. We need to hold both of these truths in tension. There is an unhealthy 'fear' of God – a fear which flows from a lack of assurance of salvation. Yet at the same time there is also an unhealthy "no fear" attitude towards God. It's not one or the other – it's both! As confusing as that sounds, we are both to fear the Lord, and to also we are told to not be afraid.

The fear of the Lord is an attitude of heart which is a result of the Spirit's presence. It cannot be manufactured in the flesh. The Holy Spirit produces the fear of the Lord. When we have the fear of the Lord in our hearts we have a deep sense of reverence and awe as we draw near to God, yet at the same time, the fear of the Lord is also the key to overcoming all other fears. The fear of the Lord will extinguish every other fear. As a result, the fear of the Lord will enable us to live a life with "no fear."

We desperately need to recover the fear of the Lord in our churches today. A recovery of the fear of the Lord will produce many other benefits. When we fear the Lord, we sin less, we are quick to repent, we will strive to live in unity, we will walk in obedience to God's commands, we will pray more fervently, we will evangelise more urgently and we will worship more reverently and authentically. The restoration of the fear of the Lord will lead us back to the normal Christian life.

Truly, God is doing a new thing in this last hour! He is restoring the apostolic and prophetic ministry functions to the Church Jesus is building. He has issued a mandate, with which the Remnant Church, the true Ekklesia, must and will comply. The Spirit has decreed it, and it must come to pass, for His Word cannot return unto Him void without accomplishing the purpose for which it is sent (Isa. 55:11). The Head of the Church, is forging change, reformation, re-formation, restructuring, to His Church. And, it IS HIS Church—to do with as He pleases, for He has purchased it with His precious shed blood. A decree for structural reformation has been issued from Heaven which cannot be negated or nullified! God will not be mocked! The Church—the TRUE Church that Jesus is building, the Remnant Church—has no choice or option in order to move forward but to hear and heed Heaven's decree and begin to comport to it.

Steve Lambert

5. A Re-aligned Church

A global pandemic that causes churches to close for an unknown period of time can be viewed as a crisis, or it can be viewed as a gift. Perhaps God is hitting the reset button. What if he is giving us the opportunity to start with a blank canvas? Many in the world are reflecting on the fact that they don't want things to go back to the madness of the way it was before; it would be crazy if the church wasn't thinking like that too. The quick adaptions that have had to be made in the last month have actually caused us to ditch a lot of the non-essential elements of church and to focus on the more essential aspects. The big question will be: can we afford to go back to 'business as usual' after this pandemic passes (assuming we have that option!)?

David Wilkerson, in his book 'The Vision' touches on how the church should respond in the midst of global shaking. He makes the following point:

> I see a kind of divine obligation to warn ministers and church organisations to take a long, hard look at all expansion programs and projects that require large sums of money. There are some building programs that must be delayed or abandoned.

The time has now come for Christian organisations to become more people-conscious than building-conscious. Most of the growth in the lean years that lie ahead should be in the areas of people-to-people ministries.

Neil Cole – a leader in the organic church movement, makes the following prediction in regards to the future of the churches post-Covid19. He says that there are three kinds of churches, and three outcomes. One church is the small struggling church. His prediction is that this church, which was only scraping by even before the pandemic, will die. However, are argues that this is actually not a bad thing. The second kind of church is the church that is a bit more business savvy. This church by means of financial gymnastics will survive. However, he argues that this is not necessarily a good thing. Why? This church hasn't learned anything. It's only goal has been to keep the machine alive. The third kind of church and outcome is the church that has adapted and as a result will be unable to go back to the way it was before. This church will have discovered some of the essential elements of true New Testament ecclesiology – and as a result, it will be unable to go back to simply maintaining the machine.

Overnight the church has been launched into a scenario that is much closer to the New Testament. We now meet for worship in our own homes – as families. After the reformation restored the gospel, and the church, it also restored family worship. It was well understood and accepted that every Christian home was a church.

In the same way that it took persecution to launch the complacent Jerusalem Christians out into mission, so it has taken a global shutdown for the church to restore the family altar.

Scotland's Bard, Robert Burns captures the spirit of those post-reformation scenes of family worship.

> The priest-like father reads the sacred page,
> How Abram was the friend of God on high;
> Or, Moses bade eternal warfare wage
> With Amalek's ungracious progeny;
> Or, how the royal Bard did groaning lie
> Beneath the stroke of Heaven's avenging ire;
> Or Job's pathetic plaint, and wailing cry;
> Or rapt Isaiah's wild, seraphic fire;
> Or other holy Seers that tune the sacred lyre.
>
> Then kneeling down to Heaven's Eternal King,
> The saint, the father, and the husband prays:
> Hope 'springs exulting on triumphant wing.'
> That thus they all shall meet in future days,
> There, ever bask in uncreated rays,
> No more to sigh or shed the bitter tear,
> Together hymning their Creator's praise,
> In such society, yet still more dear;
> While circling Time moves round in an eternal sphere.
>
> Compar'd with this, how poor Religion's pride,
> In all the pomp of method, and of art;
> When men display to congregations wide
> Devotion's ev'ry grace, except the heart,
> The Power, incens'd, the pageant will desert,
> The pompous strain, the sacerdotal stole;
> But haply, in some cottage far apart,
> May hear, well-pleas'd, the language of the soul;
> And in His Book of Life the inmates poor enroll.

Burns has clearly caught and expressed the very essence of true New Testament Christianity. The simplicity of worship in a humble home, rather than the pomp and ceremony of a grand cathedral, is much closer to the New Testament vision.

Granted – the current situation where we cannot assemble with anyone who does not live with us is a real challenge. And as good as live stream services and Zoom meetings are – they are no substitute for meeting together in person. However, the global pandemic has forced us to focus on the essential elements of Christianity – prayer, the Word, helping the vulnerable, fellowship and pastoral care. These things are far more essential than the latest program, building project, or vision that is being rolled out for our consumption.[8]

The early church was a much more simple, and yet far more powerful, entity than we see today. Sam Pascoe expressed the issue this way:

> Christianity started in Palestine as a fellowship; it moved to Greece and became a philosophy; it moved to Italy and became an institution; it moved to Europe and became a culture; it came to America and became an enterprise.

---

[8] Having said that, the lock down has neutered many essential ministries – not least evangelism, and work amongst the most vulnerable. I'm involved in a Teen Challenge Bus ministry – and that outreach has come to a complete halt. If the lockdown continues to be a long-term scenario we really need to think more seriously and creatively about how we can reach the lost (more of this in a later chapter.)

Of course, that's a bit of an oversimplification, but there is a real kernel of truth within it. The church often adopts the baggage of the culture that it finds itself in. Of course this is not how it is supposed to be. The church is supposed to transform the world; it isn't supposed to be conformed to the world.

Martin Luther King Junior described the early church in this way: "In those days the church was not merely a thermometer that recorded the ideas and principles of popular opinion; it was a thermostat that transformed the mores of society." We have to ask the question – for all our rhetoric about being "incarnational", "relational" and "seeker-sensitive" – does the emperor really have any clothes? Are we really being 'missional' or are we just deceiving ourselves? A preacher recently asked this question: If we were being put on trial for being a follower of Jesus, would there be enough evidence to convict us? Or would most of us get let off on probation?

Jesus was radical. The church is supposed to be a community of Jesus followers – how can the church be anything but radical? The problem is, we are more concerned about fitting in than standing out. We're too focused on what the church can do for us, and how it can meet our needs that we have forgotten that there are billions of people dying and going to hell.

Jesus said "Follow me." His first disciples left everything to do that. They were 100% on mission. That was their core priority. They stepped into their calling to preach the gospel, heal the sick, cast out demons and feed, clothe, and provide shelter for the poor. The needs haven't changed, neither has the calling – or the empowerment – the only thing that's changed is us. We've embraced nominalism. We must recover our radical edge as the church of Jesus Christ.

A number of years ago, whilst attending the Apostolic Church Convention in Wales, the Lord spoke to me and said "I'm re-commissioning you." Seconds later, one of the prophets began to prophesy, and he said: "The Lord is re-commissioning you." Confirmation. In the weeks that followed, I preached a sermon to the church: re-aligned for re-commissioning. In other words, as a church, I sensed the Lord was calling us to both be re-aligned, and re-commissioned. This is relevant for the western church in these days – many of our churches are attempting to carry out the work of the commission whilst not being fully aligned with the Lord's purpose. When it comes to building the church, we can't just do whatever we want – It's his house, and as a consequence, we need to build according to the pattern: "See to it that you make everything according to the pattern shown you on the mountain." (Ex. 25:40)[9]

---

[9] Berean Study Bible.

The tabernacle (God's dwelling place) had to be built according to the pattern. Moses and the people were not free to build it according to their ideas or agendas. They had to follow the pattern. Do we honestly think it is any different with the New Testament Church? This is a greater covenant. This is a house of greater glory – that means it is all the more important to build according to the pattern we see in the scriptures.

What does this mean in practice? It means we must return to church pattern as it is revealed in the New Testament – especially in the book of Acts and the letter to the Ephesians.

> So those who received his word were baptized, and there were added that day about three thousand souls. And they devoted themselves to the apostles' teaching and the fellowship, to the breaking of bread and the prayers. And awe came upon every soul, and many wonders and signs were being done through the apostles. And all who believed were together and had all things in common. And they were selling their possessions and belongings and distributing the proceeds to all, as any had need. And day by day, attending the temple together and breaking bread in their homes, they received their food with glad and generous hearts, praising God and having favor with all the people. And the Lord added to their number day by day those who were being saved.
>
> (Acts 2:41-47)

This snapshot of the young church in Acts is such a contrast to what the church has become. Notice the lack of religious liturgy and symbolism – baptism and the Lord's Supper being the only two symbols. Notice the lack of clergy/laity divide. It does not exist. Instead of a single priest, every member is a priest. Notice the lack of cathedral-like gathering, instead they gather as family, in homes.

Notice the lack of individualism – they share resources as needs arise. Notice that church is not a 'Sunday thing' – church is not a once or twice a week thing – they gather "day by day" in each other's homes. Notice the lack of religiosity, pomp and ceremony that surrounds the "breaking of bread"—it happens in the context of a meal. Notice the atmosphere – it is filled with "awe" and "praise" – this is no solemn gathering. Finally look at the power of God – signs and wonders are normative – as is the fact that people were getting saved every day. This is the church of the New Testament.

Many writers, preachers and thinkers have been raising these issues for many years. Many church leaders have helped transition their churches from an institutional machine towards a more organic and missional and organic community. Many voices have been calling for the church in the west to reform, very few have listened and responded to that call.

Now that the Lord (yes, the Lord) has shut down our religious houses, and now that many are having to adopt more biblical approaches – maybe now is the time for us to bring our churches into realignment?

In terms of re-aligning the church, Alan Hirsch makes the following observations:

> I have to admit that I always find myself shocked that after 20 centuries of Christian faith and practice in Western contexts, that still the average Christian in the average church in the West is profoundly uninformed and immature in Christ.
>
> Nowhere, perhaps, is the church's lack of formation along New Testament lines more evident than its mishandling of Apostles, Prophets, Evangelists, Pastors and Shepherds (APEST) typology.
>
> Most Christian leaders, let alone the average church attender, can give you more than two sentences to describe the apostolic or prophetic function even though these are laced throughout the scriptures. In fact the scriptures were largely birthed from within apostolic/prophetic. This glaring blind spot exposes our lack of self-awareness when it comes to the ministry and the purposes of the church and exposes fatal flaws in our discipleship, and by extension, our leadership.[10]

---

[10] Hirsch, Alan, 5Q: Reactivating the Original Intelligence and Capacity of the Body of Christ, p xxviii-xxix.

What is Hirsch saying in this extract? He is arguing that the maturity and fullness of the church in the West has been stunted because we have neglected the essential ministries that God has given for the maturing, and equipping of the church.

Ephesians chapter four clearly links the growth and well-being of the church with the ministries that Christ has given to the church: apostles, prophets, evangelists, pastors and teachers – or as some call it: the five-fold ministry.

> Therefore it says,
> "When he ascended on high he led a host of captives,
> and he gave gifts to men."
> (In saying, "He ascended," what does it mean but that he had also descended into the lower regions, the earth? He who descended is the one who also ascended far above all the heavens, that he might fill all things.) And he gave the apostles, the prophets, the evangelists, the shepherds and teachers, to equip the saints for the work of ministry, for building up the body of Christ, until we all attain to the unity of the faith and of the knowledge of the Son of God, to mature manhood, to the measure of the stature of the fullness of Christ, so that we may no longer be children, tossed to and fro by the waves and carried about by every wind of doctrine, by human cunning, by craftiness in deceitful schemes.

> Rather, speaking the truth in love, we are to grow up in every way into him who is the head, into Christ, from whom the whole body, joined and held together by every joint with which it is equipped, when each part is working properly, makes the body grow so that it builds itself up in love.
>
> (Eph. 4:8-16)

Terry Virgo also underlines the importance of these ministries in the church today.

> Can we do without apostles? The answer very much depends on what we are aiming to build. If we want to simply preserve the status quo, certainly we can cope without them. If we want a nice, cosy, charismatic house group, or a safe institutional church enjoying a little renewal now and then, we can find some of our hopes fulfilled.
>
> But if we want to see the church come to the fullness of the stature of Christ, to a mature man, it is essential for all the gifted people mentioned in Ephesians 4 to have their full place in church life.[11]

Let me conclude this chapter with a prophetic picture that a woman in our house-fellowship received last night as we gathered via Zoom to break bread and pray together. She saw that the Lord was using this season of lockdown, when all churches were closed, and his people were being called into the secret place, to re-wire the church. She said the Lord was re-wiring the church.

---

[11] Virgo, Terry, *The Spirit-Filled Church*, p152-153.

A re-wired house is a house that has greater capacity for power and electricity to be safely harnessed. I believe her vision was accurate, and I believe this re-wiring relates to the church being re-aligned to the apostolic vision which is laid out in Ephesians 4 and which is so powerfully captured in Acts 2. As we re-align our churches with the apostolic vision, we will find ourselves flowing in greater apostolic power. Why would we settle for anything less?

The Lion of Judah is arising in this hour to call forth the Greatest Harvest of Souls in modern church history. Let the Lion Roar! Change Is in the Air!
Dr. James W. Goll

And we have heard the Lion's roar, that speaks of heaven's love and power. Is this the time, is this the call, that ushers in Your kingdom rule? Oh, let the cry to nations ring, that all may come and all may sing: "Jesus is alive!" "Jesus is alive!
Matt Redman, It's Rising Up

6. The Coming Harvest

At the beginning of this book, we saw how the prophet Amos likened the Lion's roar to the prophet's warning about judgement and his call to repentance. In light of that I have argued that the Lion of Judah is roaring in the same way today. The Lord is warning us about judgement, and he is calling for repentance. However, there is another aspect of the Lion's roar, and we see it in the prophet Hosea. The lion's roar is also a call for God's people to prepare for a vast global harvest.

> They shall go after the Lord;
>   he will roar like a lion;
> when he roars,
>   his children shall come trembling from the west;
> they shall come trembling like birds from Egypt,
>   and like doves from the land of Assyria,
>   and I will return them to their homes, declares the Lord.
> (Hosea 11:10-11)

As the lion roars in judgement, in prophetic proclamation, by the preaching of the gospel, and by signs and wonders – the people shall come trembling from the East and the West. God will bring the lost home.

End Times theology is a divisive area of study within the church. There are those who argue that the end times will be marked by wide-spread evil, anti-Christ dictatorship, an apostate church and a great falling away. At the other end of the scale, there are those who argue that there will be a world-wide revival, and the Kingdom of God will manifest as never before. There seems to be scriptures for both views. Which view is correct? In my view it is both. Both are correct. The world will grow darker, but the church will also shine brighter. There will be a great apostasy, and there will be a huge harvest of souls. There will be an increase of wickedness, but there will also be a global revival. There are many scriptures which speak to this event, not least the scripture above.

> In the last days
> the mountain of the Lord's temple will be established
> > as the highest of the mountains;
> it will be exalted above the hills,
> > and peoples will stream to it.
> Many nations will come and say,
> 'Come, let us go up to the mountain of the Lord,
> > to the temple of the God of Jacob.
> He will teach us his ways,
> > so that we may walk in his paths.'
> (Micah 4:1-2)

What do we see in this glorious vision of the end times? The Lord's house: like a mountain, emerging higher than the highest of mountains. That is quite a picture.

We used to live in the highlands of Scotland. There were many glorious mountains scattered throughout the island. They could be seen from many different parts of the island. The House of God will rise in the last days with glorious mountain-like stature and grandeur! The church of God will emerge as a mountain and the nations will flock to it.

The prophet Joel, likewise speaks of an end time revival. Joel says; ""Be glad, O children of Zion, and rejoice in the LORD your God, for he has given the early rain for your vindication; he has poured down for you abundant rain, the early and the latter rain, as before." (Joel 2:23) I firmly believe that the day of Pentecost was the early rain, and before Christ returns we shall see the latter rain – a great outpouring of the Spirit that will usher in a harvest the likes of which has never been seen before.

Hugh Black, a late Scottish Pentecostal pastor, reflects on the theme of the latter rain and the last days:

> The last times started on the day of Pentecost and will end with the coming of Christ – a long period. The former rain was to fall at the beginning and the latter rain at the end of the period, as happens in the Jewish season. The early rains are required for planting seed and the floodtides of the latter rain are important for the ripening of the grain. Then comes the end: the harvest time. On the day of Pentecost, the former rains fell for the planting of the church.There were accompanying wonders – there was power and glory on the earth.

> At the end of the dispensation there will come the former and the latter rain together and with it a flood of revival—the flooding of the life of God into the church into the church, the multiplication of the saints wonderfully and gloriously. I believe that there will be a polarisation of good and evil as the end approaches.[12]

Within the church there are many sceptical believers. I've encountered many sincere believers who are cynical about almost any topic of importance. Be it revival, end-times, gifts of the Spirit, renewal, deliverance ministry, prophetic words – they are cynical. Oftentimes they lean towards a more intellectual expression of the Christian faith. To be fair, sometimes the revivalist and prophetic camps don't help the cause – there is a loony fringe that causes more sensible types to stand back and roll their eyes – but that said, we need to be careful that our faith isn't built on fleshly pride and intellectualism. We can be an astute thinker but blind to spiritual realities. It's not academic education that equips us for ministry, it's spiritual discernment.

With that being said, we need the eyes of faith to see the coming harvest. If our vision is not fixed on a harvest, then what are our eyes fixed on? The circumstances? What good will that do? Why evangelise at all if we don't expect a harvest?

---

[12] Black, Hugh, *Christian Fundamentals*, p175.

The lack of vision for the harvest probably explains the reason why there is so little evangelism going on. We don't actually expect any results. We need the Lord to open up our eyes.

> And Elijah said to Ahab, "Go up, eat and drink, for there is a sound of the rushing of rain." So Ahab went up to eat and to drink. And Elijah went up to the top of Mount Carmel. And he bowed himself down on the earth and put his face between his knees. And he said to his servant, "Go up now, look toward the sea." And he went up and looked and said, "There is nothing." And he said, "Go again," seven times. And at the seventh time he said, "Behold, a little cloud like a man's hand is rising from the sea." And he said, "Go up, say to Ahab, 'Prepare your chariot and go down, lest the rain stop you.'" And in a little while the heavens grew black with clouds and wind, and there was a great rain. And Ahab rode and went to Jezreel. And the hand of the Lord was on Elijah, and he gathered up his garment and ran before Ahab to the entrance of Jezreel.
>
> (1 Kings 18:41-46)

Elijah could hear the sound of rain before there was even a cloud in the sky. How is that possible? Elijah was moving in the prophetic. When we move in the prophetic, we are not moved by the five senses. We don't walk by sight, we walk by faith. The prophetic anointing will enable us to hear things that others can't, and see things that others can't.

Why was the world condemned when Noah and his family weren't? Noah heard and saw what others could not. He heard the rain before it fell. As the people of God, we are called to walk in the light, we should never be caught off guard. We should be prepared for anything. If judgement is around the corner, those who are dwelling in the secret place, with the Lord, will not be caught off guard. If revival is about to be poured out, those who are walking with God will not be caught of guard – on the contrary, they will prepare the way for it. Just as John the Baptist – the last Old Testament prophet, knew that Jesus was here, before others did, and prepared the way for the Lord, so we too are called to prepare the way for his coming. We are called to prepare the way for the coming outpouring of the Spirit, and we are called to prepare the way for the coming harvest. Can you hear the sound of rain? Can you hear the lion's roar? Can you see the vision of the coming harvest?

As exciting as it is to reflect on a coming harvest, it's important to remember that prior to a harvest, the fallow ground needs to be broken up, seeds need to be sown, rains need to fall, and there is a time of patient waiting – then comes the harvest. Hosea said: "Sow for yourselves righteousness; reap steadfast love; break up your fallow ground, for it is the time to seek the LORD, that he may come and rain righteousness upon you." (Hosea 10:12)

And Jeremiah said: "For thus says the LORD to the men of Judah and Jerusalem: "Break up your fallow ground, and sow not among thorns."

Charles Finney helps us get to grips with what it means to break up our fallow ground.

> To break up the fallow ground, is to break up your hearts, to prepare your minds to bring forth fruit unto God. The mind of man is often compared to the ground in the bible. The Word of God is the seed sown there, the fruit representing the actions and emotions of those who receive it. To break up the fallow ground therefore, is to bring the mind into such a state that it is fitted to receive the Word of God. Sometimes your hearts get matted down, hard and dry, until there is no such thing as getting fruit from them until they are broken up, and mellowed down, and fitted to the Word. It is this softening of the heart, so as to make it feel the truth, which the prophet calls breaking up your fallow ground.

We mustn't only think of revival as God's presence coming upon us – although it is that too. We must remember that revival is within us because the Spirit of revival is within us. The problem is not at the source, the problem is with the vessel. Our hearts are too clogged up. We need to plough up the fallow ground of our hearts.

Breaking up the fallow ground of our hearts is one of the things the Lord wants to do in us during this lockdown period.

With so many of our distractions stripped away – cinemas, restaurants, gyms, etc. we have an opportunity to rediscover the secret place. As we draw near to him, and align our lives more fully with his will and purpose – we are preparing the way for revival. We are becoming vessels that can carry revival.

A Christian leader recently sent a prayer request out to a group of believers on a social media app. The update said something like this: *by the time we get a vaccine it will be too late, by the time the economy opens again, it will be too late, the damage will already be done – we need to pray for a miracle so that the economy can open again quickly.*

My response was less than diplomatic. I responded by saying that it is more important that we pray for global repentance because if things were to turn around overnight, and we were to go back to the way things were – we will have missed God's purpose in this lockdown. God has given us a gift of grace – the opportunity to see the futility of our way of life, and the chance to come to repentance. The church also has a second chance – we have a second chance to get our hearts ready for revival. It's time to fix our eyes on the harvest.

You say, don't you, "In four more months the harvest will begin?' Look, I tell you, open your eyes and observe that the fields are ready for harvesting now![13] *(John 4:35)*

---

[13] NIV.

I have seen whole countries shaken by the power of God.
Reinhard Bonnke

Every single, solitary soul is precious.
Reinhard Bonnke

7. Rescue the Lost

"Preaching the gospel isn't going to cut it."

These were the words of wisdom that were shared a few days ago on a denominational Facebook group by a renowned Biblical Scholar. It was all part of a dialogue about how wonderful a job he's doing connecting with unbelievers and introducing them to monasticism. Of course it was all couched in language about how sensitive he is to the millennial culture – and how it's all about listening and telling stories to a group of people who "don't want to be told how it is." Of course the irony is he is lecturing everyone on Facebook, not doing much listening, and telling us all how it is.

This example is not an isolated incident, many churches in the West have been shaped by their theological institutions – and many of the theological institutions have sold out to secular values. In their pursuit of secular accreditation, many have sold their birth-right.

Sadly, it seems that a number of theological institutions are more focused on raising maintainers of the ecclesiastical machine, than releasing prophets and pioneers into the harvest field.

As a result they have a professional clergy lecturing students about how the gospel isn't relevant and how we all need to go back to lighting candles, mimicking monks, and reciting some ancient religious liturgy.

Sorry – but maybe this kind of religious activity scratches the itch of disenfranchised evangelicals who were raised in church by their parents who were raised in church by their parents who were also raised in church, but I wasn't raised in church, I was raised in some of the toughest and poorest streets in Scotland – and it was an encounter with the risen Christ that transformed me, not some recycled and regurgitated religion from back in a time when Monks sat in silence and didn't even obey the call to preach the gospel to all creation. No wonder the religious evangelical establishment wants to return to monasticism – a silent religion is all they are comfortable with.

Preaching the gospel doesn't cut it? Tell that to the apostle Paul who declared: "For if I preach the gospel, that gives me no ground for boasting. For necessity is laid upon me. Woe to me if I do not preach the gospel!" (1 Cor. 9:16) Preaching the gospel doesn't cut it? Tell that to the Apostle proclaimed: "For I am not ashamed of the gospel, for it is the power of God for salvation to everyone who believes, to the Jew first and also to the Greek." (Romans 1:16)

On the contrary, preaching the gospel – when done in faith, love, and anointing will absolutely cut it. Like Peter on the day of Pentecost – it will cut the hearers to the hearts.

The problem is not that 'preaching the gospel does not cut it', the problem is that too few preachers have been cut by the preaching of the gospel.

One of the realities that has struck me during this pandemic is the fact that the whole world is more or less under the equivalent of house arrest, the economy has shut down, the media are preaching fear, the masses are unsettled and most of the church is sitting at home watching Netflix, or making Tik Tok videos. Okay – so most church leaders have done a crash course on live streaming and they are putting their services online. But what about the majority of unbelievers who aren't tuning into live streamed church services? Who is going to reach the people on their way to the chemist or the supermarket if you or I don't?

I live in a rural village; there are not too many people around. That was even true before the lockdown. However on the two occasions that I've had to go into the city centre, I've been compelled to preach the gospel. I've never felt the streets so thick with fear. I've never seen people looking so haunted. How could I walk amongst these people and not preach the gospel?

"Did it work?" That's what people always ask. Yet such questions just show that they don't understand the principle of sowing and reaping. I sowed seed. I pierced the atmosphere with the name of Jesus. I called people to repentance and declared with urgency the reality that 'The King is coming – we need to get ready!'

I'll hold off to the day of judgement to find out if it worked.

Of course I love it when I get to bring in the harvest. Of course it's great when you reap. But we're called to preach the gospel – leave the results up to the Holy Spirit.

Do I not realise that preaching the gospel in the middle of a city centre looks nuts? Of course I do. I'm not an idiot. But here's the thing – when I surrendered my life to Christ at the turn of the millennium – I died to self. My reputation died that day. I gave my all to Jesus Christ. Consequently – I'm willing to look like a fool, in order that I may save some. If some person happens to get gripped by the Spirit deep in their hearts as I'm preaching the gospel like a loony on the streets and that person walks by but for the next few days is haunted by the Holy Spirit until he bows the knee to Jesus – I'm happy. I believe the Bible – and the Bible tells me that "faith comes by hearing, and hearing by the Word of Christ."

I appreciate that not every Christian is an evangelist. But I also believe the Bible when it tells me that the five-fold ministries are given to equip the church. That tells me that part of the role of the evangelist is to provoke the church to do evangelism.

I don't think the fundamental issue is a lack of skills. That's what we assume as Westerners: "Oh, we need to be trained how to reach people."

What this usually means is we want some kind of programme that helps us feel comfortable and qualified. No – I don't think it's a lack of training. I think the problem is fear and pride. Most middle-class Christian professionals are, for most of their lives, in their comfort zones. They don't like being made to feel like they can't do something. When it comes to winning the lost – they are terrified – terrified of rejection, terrified of failing, terrified of not knowing what to say. They're also deeply proud. They don't want to feel incompetent. Feel incompetent – you are, and when it comes to being used by God, incompetence is the perfect qualification. Be afraid – it's actually how we should be: "And I was with you in weakness and in fear and much trembling." (1 Cor. 2:3) Don't know much? Good – knowledge is a hindrance, be like Paul: "For I decided to know nothing among you except Jesus Christ and him crucified." (1 Cor. 2:2)

I really think there are only two fundamental issues that we need to resolve within ourselves: the first is to feel deep compassion for the lost – people outside of Christ are going to hell, and the second is to believe that the message of the gospel has the power to save them and that is why they must hear it –and that is why we must share it!

Of course there is more to it than this – not least the need for prayer, and a baptism of the Holy Spirit and power (that's the next chapter) – but these two issues are foundation stones, and they are foundation stones that are missing in the lives of too many believers.

Too many have lost confidence in the power of the gospel.

Maybe part of the issue is that we have lost sight of hell. William Booth, the great soul winner, social activist, revivalist and founder of the Salvation Army once said that he wishes the final part of training for his people could be for them to be dangled over hell for 5 minutes. This was not to make them fearful of going there – their destiny is heaven. It was to help the see the horrors that await those who don't know Christ. A vision of hell should awaken deep compassion within the church for the lost. If we have no compassion for the lost, it is because we are blind to the eternal torment of hell. William Booth put it this way:

Most Christians would like to send their recruits to Bible college for five years. I would like to send them to hell for five minutes. That would do more than anything else to prepare them for a lifetime of compassionate ministry.

> For those believers who would claim that they are not called to reach the lost, Booth said this:
>
> Not called! did you say?
>
> 'Not heard the call,' I think you should say.
>
> Put your ear down to the Bible, and hear Him bid you go and pull sinners out of the fire of sin. Put your ear down to the burdened, agonized heart of humanity, and listen to its pitiful wail for help.
>
> Go stand by the gates of hell, and hear the damned entreat you to go to their father's house and bid their brothers and sisters and servants and masters not to come there.
>
> Then look Christ in the face - whose mercy you have professed to obey - and tell Him whether you will join heart and soul and body and circumstances in the march to publish His mercy to the world.

In an earlier chapter, I asked you if you have ever felt the Bible's teaching on hell. I asked if you had ever come under a deep, traumatic sobering conviction about the final judgement. If you haven't, I really believe you need to seek the Lord. How can you claim Jesus as your saviour if you don't have the faintest sense of what he has saved you from?

The horrors of Calvary are a glimpse into the depth of our wickedness and the severity of God's wrath.

However, if you have felt the sting of hell, how can you remain indifferent to the lost, knowing that is their fate? Has it been so long since you experienced the sense of God's wrath that you have forgotten? Have you numbed your spiritual sensitivity because you've been overdosing on songs of sweet assurance? Have you not read in the prophets: "Woe to those who are at ease in Zion, and to those who feel secure on the mountain of Samaria, the notable men of the first of the nations, to whom the house of Israel comes!"? (Amos 6:1)

Have we become "at ease in Zion?" When I first became a Christian, one of the old Brethren preachers I knew used to have a phrase: "I'm saved and satisfied." Most contemporary Christians don't even use language about being saved these days, but many still have the spirit of being satisfied. How can we be satisfied? If anything, knowing Christ should birth a longing within us – a longing to know him more fully and a longing for the lost to be found.

Maybe it's been too long since we visited the scriptures that reveal the nature of eternal judgement. Read these verses prayerfully, asking the Lord to give you a new burden for the lost.

> And do not fear those who kill the body but cannot kill the soul. Rather fear him who can destroy both soul and body in hell. (Matt. 10:28)

Then he will say to those on his left, 'Depart from me, you cursed, into the eternal fire prepared for the devil and his angels. (Matt.25:41)

But I say to you that everyone who is angry with his brother will be liable to judgment; whoever insults his brother will be liable to the council; and whoever says, 'You fool!' will be liable to the hell of fire. (Matt. 5:22)

And throw them into the fiery furnace. In that place there will be weeping and gnashing of teeth. (Matt.13:50)

And if your hand causes you to sin, cut it off. It is better for you to enter life crippled than with two hands to go to hell, to the unquenchable fire.

And if your foot causes you to sin, cut it off. It is better for you to enter life lame than with two feet to be thrown into hell. And if your eye causes you to sin, tear it out. It is better for you to enter the kingdom of God with one eye than with two eyes to be thrown into hell, 'where their worm does not die and the fire is not quenched.' (Mark 9:43-48)

And many of those who sleep in the dust of the earth shall awake, some to everlasting life, and some to shame and everlasting contempt. (Dan.12:2)

His winnowing fork is in his hand, and he will clear his threshing floor and gather his wheat into the barn, but the chaff he will burn with unquenchable fire." (Matt.3:12)

Whoever believes in the Son has eternal life; whoever does not obey the Son shall not see life, but the wrath of God remains on him. (John. 3:36)

> While the sons of the kingdom will be thrown into the outer darkness. In that place there will be weeping and gnashing of teeth." (Matt. 8:12)
>
> Wild waves of the sea, casting up the foam of their own shame; wandering stars, for whom the gloom of utter darkness has been reserved forever. (Jude. 1:13)
>
> He also will drink the wine of God's wrath, poured full strength into the cup of his anger, and he will be tormented with fire and sulfur in the presence of the holy angels and in the presence of the Lamb. (Rev. 14:10)
>
> And the smoke of their torment goes up forever and ever, and they have no rest, day or night, these worshipers of the beast and its image, and whoever receives the mark of its name." (Rev. 14:11)
>
> And if anyone's name was not found written in the book of life, he was thrown into the lake of fire. (Rev. 20:15)

These are sobering texts. In the natural, they strong words with vivid imagery. Yet only the Holy Spirit can illuminate our hearts to something of their reality. Even then, we only get a small glimpse – the full reality of hell is too much for anyone to grasp. This is what makes it so terrible.

We must also remember that it is not God's desire to send anyone to hell. He gave his Son to be crucified in order to save us from hell. The Lamb of God died so that the wrath of God would pass over us. Our salvation is free but it came at a great cost – the cross of our Lord Jesus Christ.

In light of these texts about hell, Charles Finney (a tremendous evangelist) offers the following guidance to help us maintain our cutting edge in reaching the lost. Finney says we should:

- See that you are constrained by love to preach the gospel, as Christ was to provide a gospel.
- See that you have the special enduement of power from on high, by the baptism of the Holy Ghost.
- Constantly maintain a close walk with God.
- Make the Bible your book of books. Study it much, upon your knees, waiting for divine light.
- See that you have a heart, and not merely a head call to undertake the preaching of the gospel. By this I mean, be heartily and most intensely inclined to seek the salvation of souls as the great work of life, and do not undertake what you have no heart to.
- Contemplate much the guilt and danger of sinners, that your zeal for their salvation may be intensified.
- Also deeply ponder and dwell much upon the boundless love and compassion of Christ for them.
- So love them yourself as to be willing to die for them.

- Give your most intense thought to the study of ways and means by which you may save them. Make this the great and intense study of your life.
- Refuse to be diverted from this work. Guard against every temptation that would abate your interest in it.
- Believe the assertion of Christ that He is with you in this work always and everywhere, to give you all the help you need.
- Spend much time every day and night in prayer and direct communion with God. (No amount of learning and study can compensate for the loss of this communion.)
- Let all your sermons be heart and not merely head sermons.
- Preach from experience, and not from hearsay, or mere reading and study.
- Be full of prayer whenever you attempt to preach, and go from your closet to your pulpit with the inward groanings of the Spirit pressing for utterance at your lips.
- See that "the fear of man that bringeth a snare" is not upon you. Let your people understand that you fear God too much to be afraid of them
- See that you personally know and daily live upon Christ.

Could you feel the piercing of the Holy Spirit as you read Finney's guidelines? The one that got me was: "So love them yourself as to be willing to die for them." Wow! Forgive us Lord for even contemplating to reach the lost before we even love them. I have to be honest, I'm not there. Are you? Would you be willing to give up your salvation, and suffer an eternity in hell, in order that others might be saved? Paul was:

> I am speaking the truth in Christ—I am not lying; my conscience bears me witness in the Holy Spirit— that I have great sorrow and unceasing anguish in my heart. For I could wish that I myself were accursed and cut off from Christ for the sake of my brothers, my kinsmen according to the flesh. (Rom. 9:1-3)

This is the Spirit of God who has inspired these words. Yet Paul was so filled with the Spirit that he could love like Christ. Christ was cast off and accursed for our sakes. The love of Christ has so transformed Paul that he would die for the lost. No wonder he was such an effective evangelist – he was motivated by the love of Christ. May we too be so transformed by the love of Christ that we are willing to take this message of salvation to everyone we can whilst there is time.

When you strip it of everything else, Pentecost stands for power and life. That's what came into the church when the Holy Spirit came down on the day of Pentecost.
David Wilkerson

Pentecost came with the sound of a mighty rushing wind, a violent blast from heaven! Heaven has not exhausted its blasts, but our danger is we are getting frightened of them.
Smith Wigglesworth

There is only one purpose of Pentecost; that is to effectively evangelize lost souls.
T.L. Osborn

8. A Baptism of the Holy Spirit & Fire

If the Holy Spirit was withdrawn from the church today, 95 percent of what we do would go on and no one would know the difference. If the Holy Spirit had been withdrawn from the New Testament church, 95 percent of what they did would stop, and everybody would know the difference." A.W. Tozer

These words from Tozer should stop us in our tracks. Discerning believers feel the truth of this. It is impossible to not see the contrast between the church in the book of Acts and the 21st century Western church. In fact the church has become so comfortable with the lack of supernatural that we have developed a theology to support it. We call it cessationism.

The Spirit of God is mentioned 88 times in the Old Testament, he is mentioned 264 times in the New Testament, there are 60+ references in the Gospels, 57 references to the Spirit in Acts, and he is mentioned 132 times in the epistles.

There is no question that the Holy Spirit is central in the life of the New Testament church, yet somehow we have placed him on the substitute's bench, preferring instead our programs, our doctrines, our traditions and our human creativity.

Surely the neglect of the Holy Spirit is one of the greatest scandals of the 21st century church?

The purpose of this chapter is not to study every aspect of the Holy Spirit – an impossible task! Our focus is the baptism of the Holy Spirit. Before we discuss this further, let's look at some of the essential things the New Testament says about the baptism in the Spirit.

John the Baptist prophesied both the coming of Jesus and the nature of his work. Interestingly, baptism with the Holy Spirit is mentioned at the start. From this it is clear the baptism of the Spirit is not some kind of secondary issue – it is foundational to what Jesus came to do.

> I baptize you with water for repentance, but he who is coming after me is mightier than I, whose sandals I am not worthy to carry. He will baptize you with the Holy Spirit and fire. (Matt. 3:11)

Jesus himself, after his resurrection, and prior to the ascension, also stressed the importance of the coming Spirit. The disciples were commissioned to go and preach the gospel and make disciples of all nations – but they were clearly instructed not to do this before they were empowered by the Holy Spirit.

> And behold, I am sending the promise of my Father upon you. But stay in the city until you are clothed with power from on high." (Luke 24:49)

The disciples knew their scriptures. They would know the Old Testament accounts about the Holy Spirit coming upon servants of God in the past. Their minds may have turned to the Spirit's work on David, or Samson or one of the other Old Testament giants. Perhaps they would have thought about the words of the Old Testament prophet, Samuel as he spoke to Saul:

> Then the Spirit of the LORD will rush upon you, and you will prophesy with them and be turned into another man. (1 Sam. 10:6)

This is very powerful, notice three things: the Spirit would "rush" on him, he would prophesy, and he would be changed into a different person. It needs to be said, this is not a 'unique' work of the Spirit – it is not abnormal – this is the normal pattern. These three aspects are central to what the Spirit does when he comes upon a person. This is exactly what happened on the day of Pentecost.

> When the day of Pentecost arrived, they were all together in one place. And suddenly there came from heaven a sound like a mighty rushing wind, and it filled the entire house where they were sitting. And divided tongues as of fire appeared to them and rested on each one of them. And they were all filled with the Holy Spirit and began to speak in other tongues as the Spirit gave them utterance. (Acts 2:3-4)

Notice the "rushing wind" – just like the "rush" that Samuel mentioned. Notice the Spirit-inspired speech – only this time it is the gift of tongues, and not prophesy (elsewhere in Acts, when the Spirit comes there is both tongues and prophecies). Finally, consider the effects of this experience upon the disciples – they were changed into new men and women. They were not the same. They were transformed from timid, fearful cowards into bold, joy-filled prophets.

And this is exactly what the Old Testament predicted would happen when the ascended Christ would pour out his Spirit. Peter himself explains the account, on the day of Pentecost, by referring to the prophet Joel.

> And afterward, I will pour out my Spirit on all people. Your sons and daughters will prophesy, your old men will dream dreams, your young men will see visions. (Joel 2:28)

Again, notice the link between poured out Spirit, and prophetic experience. The two are inseparable. Yet for some reason this is not the case in much of what passes for contemporary Christianity. We'll pay lip-service to the Spirit – and we'll tell everyone how gentle, and quiet he is – we've even dared to claim that he is "the silent member of the Godhead." What drivel! What blasphemy. If the Spirit is silent, it is because we have silenced him – and his silence is not a sign of his presence, it's a sign of his judgement.

In order to justify the ecclesiastical gagging of the Spirit of God, we've justified his silence with centuries upon centuries of institutional theology. We've claimed such an experience was only for the apostles. The coming of the Spirit in power was only to kick start the church. Now that Christendom has expanded the globe, and the canon is complete, and we've crystallised our creeds there is no need for this kind of encounter. Church instead is more normative, more rational, less emotional, and less supernatural. Yet there is one simple piece of evidence that exposes this view for the myth that it is – revival. Revival. That's right, every now and again the Holy Spirit comes storming out of the naughty corner! He breaks out from the box that we've placed him in. In other words, the evidence of the on-going ministry of the Holy Spirit is there for all to see.

Right now the Spirit of God is moving all over the globe. As cessationist preachers are delivering their 12 point sermons explaining why dreams and visions have ceased, the Spirit of God is visiting Muslims in the middle of the night with glorious dreams and visions of the exalted Son of God. As conservative pastors desperately try to control the spirituality of the people, the Spirit of God is pouring out the gift of tongues and prophecy upon ordinary believers in their denomination.

In the same way that we can't stop the rain falling from the sky, or the wind blowing, or the sub shining, neither can we stop the moving of the Spirit of God.

You may choose to put up an umbrella or go and hide in a locked room, but he will continue to fall like rain, rush like the wind, and shine like the sun!

Let us now turn to some of these powerful post-biblical era examples of the baptism of the Holy Spirit.

Earlier we looked at the effects that the baptism in the Holy Spirit had upon the revivalist Charles Finney, now let us look at his description of his experience of being baptised with the Holy Spirit.

> I was powerfully converted on the morning of the tenth of October. In the evening of the same day and on the morning of the following day, I received overwhelming baptisms of the Holy Spirit, which went through me, as it seemed to me, body and soul. I immediately found myself clothed with such power from on high that a few words dropped here and there to individuals were the means of their immediate conversion. My words seemed to fasten like barbed arrows in the souls of men. They cut like a sword. They broke the heart like a hammer. Multitudes can attest to this. Oftentimes, a word dropped, without my remembering it, would fasten conviction and often result in an almost immediate conversion.

Just like the apostles, Finney's encounter with the Spirit followed his conversion. It didn't happen at the exact same time. We don't need to be rigid about this. There are examples in scripture where there is a delay between conversion and the empowering of the Spirit, and there are examples of the Spirit falling at the same time.

The important thing is that believers push through until they are empowered.

Also look at Finney's description of the experience – he felt it – it affected his whole being. Finally, look at the effects, like the early apostles, his preaching was transformed. God's presence accompanied his testimony about Christ, the result being, those who heard were affected. This is exactly what Jesus described – power to be a witness.

Charles Fox Parham is credited by *some* historians as being the founder of Pentecostalism. While not developing his own views in a vacuum, he seems to be responsible for pioneering the Pentecostal doctrine of 'Baptism with the Holy Spirit with tongues as the initial evidence'.

Whilst most evangelicals would have little difficulty with accepting the signs of powerful witnessing as evidence of the work of the Holy Spirit, many have difficulty when it comes to other signs such as tongues and prophecy. Yet despite conservative caution, the Holy Spirit has saw fit to move in power in fresh Pentecostal power time and time again. The church has often found these aspects of his ministry embarrassing, but that hasn't stopped the Holy Spirit resurrecting these signs of his presence.

Charles Fox Parham started Bethel Bible School in Kansas in 1898. In the December of 1900 Parham asked his students to study the bible and discover one sign that demonstrated the evidence of Spirit Baptism.

Parham then left for three days and arrived to find that the students unanimously believed that the only initial evidence of Baptism with the Holy Spirit was speaking in other tongues.[14]

On New Year's eve an all-night service was held for prayer, presumably to seek the baptism of the Spirit). During this service Agnes Ozman approached Parham, saying that she felt Parham was to lay hands on her according to the scripture that she may be baptised in the Holy Spirit. Apparently Parham was reluctant to do this however he eventually agreed.

> Sister Agnes N. Ozman (now LaBerge) asked that hands might be laid upon her to receive the Holy Spirit as she hoped to go to foreign fields. At first I refused not having the experience myself. Then being further pressed to do it humbly in the name of Jesus, I laid my hand upon her head and prayed. I had scarcely repeated three dozen sentences when a glory fell upon her, a halo seemed to surround her head and face, and she began speaking in the Chinese language, and was unable to speak English for three days. [15]

---

[14] Synan, *100 Years*, p44.

[15] William K. Kay, Anne Dyer, *Reader: Pentecostal and Charismatic Studies* (London, SCM Press, 2004) p11.

Ozman was the first of Parham's students to enter into this experience, yet this event was catalystic. Such was the impact of what happened to Agnes Ozman that day has been referred to as 'a touch felt around the world'.[16]

Since that time the global Pentecostal and charismatic movements have shaken the globe. In countries were Christians are persecuted for their faith, the Spirit continues to pour out his presence with signs following. The question of whether speaking in tongues is *the* essential, or *only*, "evidence" that a person has been baptised in the Holy Spirit has almost become irrelevant. The fact is when he comes "stuff happens." His presence is felt, he transforms individuals, he empowers weak believers and fills them with boldness, he heals, and he pours out the gifts of prophecy and tongues. It might not fit with some people's theology, but he doesn't seem too bothered by that.

Whilst the outpouring of the Spirit at the turn of the 20th century has brought tremendous revival and renewal in many places, it has not been without its problems --one problem being the institutionalisation of the movement.

Mark Driscoll once made the point that God will raise up a man who will spark a movement but the movement will then become an institution, and the institution will become a monument and finally the monument will become a museum.

---

[16] Synan, 100 years, p1.

Pentecostalism is no different. Many Pentecostal denominations and churches have completed the transition from movement to museum and as a result, just like all the other dead denominations have become as religious, cold, and traditional as the churches that once kicked out the Pentecostals.

Of course, like many denominations, many Pentecostal churches have developed an appearance of life – there is vibrant music, technological advancement that creates trailers for church services that feel as exciting as a blockbuster movie, there is activity, and life and laughter – but is there power? Is there the manifestation of his presence? Do our services reflect those early days of outpouring? Or have we substituted The Spirit of God for gimmicks?

Hugh Black touches on this issue:

> There are young people who come to a point where they seek the baptism of the Holy Spirit and they speak a few words in tongues and disappear off the face of the earth—gone. Why?...We are waiting to see the burning of fire—to hear the powerful delivery of the word of God, to the salvation of souls...We are seeing no burning fire, no blazing prairie. We are not hearing of people being convicted of sin...Is it any wonder that some people say, 'Is that Pentecost? Is that the Acts two experience? Is it for real?'

> Squinty Pentecost...Real Pentecost is an encounter with the divine, and it explodes a man- and if a man is not exploded he should examine himself to see that he has received the fullness of his birth-right.

> If your life is in no wise changed in the hour of conversion, you are not converted, and if your life is in no wise changed in the hour of baptism in the Spirit go back and again and seek God.[17]

In drawing this chapter to a close, let me return to one of the scriptures we looked at earlier: Then the Spirit of the LORD will rush upon you, and you will prophesy with them and be turned into another man. (1 Sam. 10:6) Can we honestly say that we have experienced this? We're not just talking about goosebumps during the latest Bethel song. Has he rushed upon you? Has his presence manifested in Spirit-inspired speech – be it tongues or prophecy. Have you been deeply changed? These are the marks of the Spirit of God.

Let me finish with a question that Paul once asked a group of religious seekers: "'And he said to them, "Did you receive the Holy Spirit when you believed?" And they said, "No, we have not even heard that there is a Holy Spirit."' (Acts 19:2) Well? Did you? How do you know? When you professed Christ, did his Spirit rush upon you? Have you found yourself anointed to speak about the things of Christ?

Have you received the gift of tongues? Are you moving in the prophetic? Have you been deeply changed? If not, perhaps you need to seek God for the fullness of the Spirit.

---

[17] Hugh Black, *Christian Fundamentals*, (Scotland, New Dawn, 1991) p29-33.

Why not take a moment to pray the following prayer – but before you do, be sure to spend time in repentance.

You may want to repent for neglecting the Holy Spirit, but you should also confess any known sin and plead the blood for forgiveness. Purity is a condition for power –first the blood, then the fire. Once you have confessed your sins, received forgiveness, and surrendered afresh to God, you should pray this prayer.

Heavenly Father, at this moment I come to you. I thank you that Jesus saved me. I pray that the Holy Spirit might come upon me. Lord Jesus, baptise me now in the Holy Spirit. I receive the baptism in the Holy Spirit right now by faith in Your Word. May the anointing, the glory, and the power of God come upon me and into my life right now. May I be empowered for service from this day forward. Thank You, Lord Jesus, for baptising me in Your Holy Spirit. Amen.

Long-lasting victory can never be separated from a long-lasting stand on the foundation of the cross.

Watchman Nee

"If we understand that everything happening to us is to make us more Christ-like, it will solve a great deal of anxiety in our lives."

A.W. Tozer, The Crucified Life: How To Live Out A Deeper Christian Experience

9. Resurrecting the Crucified Life

"It is one thing to read about being filled with the Holy Spirit and quite another thing to experience the mighty infilling of the Holy Spirit that radically changes our life to a life of adoring wonder and amazement at the things of God. Reading and experiencing are two quite different things."

— A.W. Tozer, The Crucified Life: How To Live Out A Deeper Christian Experience

Despite the global impact of the Pentecostal and charismatic movements, there is still a great divorce taking place within the church. Two essential marks of the Holy Spirit are gifts and godliness. Sadly, people are often more interested in the excitement that surrounds the gifts than they are about the godliness that the Spirit desires to produce.

There can be no separation though. Any Holy Spirit movement that does not strike at the root of sin and transform our character – no matter how much noise it makes, no matter how many revelations and visions it claims – is not a genuine work of the Spirit.

The Spirit is interested in both power and purity, but I think he is more interested in purity. Power without purity is dangerous. Gifts without godliness is a risky path.

We must never separate the need for the gifts of the Spirit from the need for the fruit of the Holy Spirit. Samson is a lesson to us in this regard. Samson was a man who operated in the anointing, but he played fast and loose with God. He flirted with the devil and it cost him everything. Many anointed ministries have been shipwrecked because they thought they could move in the anointing by day, and sleep with the devil at night. God may allow such ministries to carry on for a season, but if there is no repentance there will be a train-wreck. It's only a matter of time.

As I write these words I am thinking of a certain revivalist ministry that is well-known globally. This revivalist seemed to explode on the scene. There were weekly televised revival meetings. The crowds gathered. The money flowed. And no sooner had he peaked when all of a sudden it came crashing down. There was a moral failure – adultery, drunkenness, divorce – chaos.

Anyone can sin. After a period of restoration, the revivalist is back up and running. Yet, it seems that there has just been one moral tragedy after another. Whistle-blowers within his ministry have reported a number of sexual scandals dating back many years. It seems clear, there is a pattern of sin. This time it seems the ministry has come crashing down. Supporters have bailed out. Yet the revivalist continues – his live streams are still being churned out. Despite the fact that his live viewers seem to have dropped from thousands to a handful, the revivalist continues.

Listening to him is a sad experience. The fire has died, and all that's left is a desperate man trying to reignite the fire that's long died. More time is spent desperately appealing for donations and trying to sell old teaching products than is spent carrying fire, passion and words of life. The fire is gone, but the religious show continues. I'm not judging him. God have mercy on us all. There but for the grace of God go I – but I'm stressing a point, we can't play with Holy Fire and flirt with the devil's pleasures – we will get burnt.

Many conservative believers point at the number of moral scandals that take place within the charismatic movement and use it as ammunition against the gifts of the Spirit. I mean how can the movement be of God when there are so many scandals? Firstly I'd respond by pointing to the New Testament – the churches had many scandals, particularly in Corinth. Corinth is a very charismatic church, but it was also full of sin. Yet Paul affirmed them in the gifts, yes he corrected excesses, but he affirmed their experience of the gifts and he rebuked them for their immorality. We should be like Paul – we want the gifts and godliness, we want power and purity.

Secondly we need to note that ministry scandals are not just in the domain of the charismatic movement – sin is no respecter of denominations.

A number of years ago I was pastoring a small Presbyterian church in the central belt, as an elder I was commissioned to attend the denomination's General Assembly in Edinburgh. It was one of the most solemn and sobering experiences of my life. One of the movement's spiritual giants had died by suicide. Following the news of the suicide were a multitude of allegations of sexual perversion and adultery spanning back decades. The investigation into these matters took place during that assembly, the one and only assembly that I ever attended. The assembly judged that the allegations were true. The event shook me to the core. The weightiness and seriousness of the call to ministry, and the dangers of sin and vulnerability of human nature was etched upon my heart and mind at that assembly. The saying is true: *sin will take you places you do not want to go, make you stay longer than you want to stay, and make you pay more than you want to pay.* God have mercy.

There is a tendency for the church to focus on the wrong things. We tend to emphasise the wrong things. We highlight the positive aspects of the Christian faith, but we overlook the more challenging aspects. As a result we actually dilute the positive aspects. The love of God is sweeter and more powerful when we understand it in light of his holiness and wrath. Forgiveness of sin is sweeter when we understand just how wicked sin is and how much it is hated by a holy God.

One aspect of biblical teaching that seems to have slipped out of sight is the teaching of the crucified life. The apostle Paul wrote: "I have been crucified with Christ. It is no longer I who live, but Christ who lives in me. And the life I now live in the flesh I live by faith in the Son of God, who loved me and gave himself for me." (Gal,2:20) This is revolutionary teaching, It's teaching that changed my life.

Too often, discipleship is viewed us self-improvement. It's almost assumed that we just have to make certain lifestyle adjustments. Nothing could be further from the truth. We are not called to change ourselves, we are called to die.

The revivalist musician, Keith Green once noted:

> Paul said, "I determined to know nothing among you except Jesus Christ, and Him crucified." (1Co 2:2) Nowadays it's "Jesus Christ and what He can do for you!" You cannot have more exact opposites than the Bible's Christ-centered Gospel,(Matt 10:38; Luk 14:27; 1Co 1:17-18; Gal 6:14; Eph 2:6; Col 1:20; 1Pe 2:24) and our modern, cross-less, me-centered gospel.
>
> Today, if anyone preaches self-denial as a condition of discipleship, you can hear the comments afterwards: "old-fashioned," "harsh," "legalistic." I dare say that our Lord would have as much trouble finding acceptance among our preachers as He had among the religious leaders of His own day.

However – this message of the crucified life can be misunderstood.

I do not have to crucify myself; I've already been crucified with Christ. That's what Paul teaches. When? 2000 years ago. What we need to do is enter into that which Christ has done for us – this too is a work of the Holy Spirit, and like our justification – it happens by faith and faith alone. How can I experience victory over my lusts, my temper, and my sinful habits? In the same way that I trusted Christ for justification – I simply believe. As I believed in his grace alone for forgiveness, so I now must believe that his cross has delivered me from the power of sin. The cross does not only remove the guilt and penalty of my sins, it delivers me from the power of sin.

David Wilkerson is helpful here, and is worth quoting at length.

> Now, how do we get Jesus' victory and power in our own lives? How do we appropriate his resurrection and newness of life?
>
> First, let me ask you: How do you know you are saved? It is by faith alone, of course. The word declares we are to consider ourselves alive unto God. The knowledge of our salvation comes by our faith alone in God's word.
>
> Likewise, we are to take up the cross, embrace it and receive victory by faith in the overcoming power of Jesus' shed blood. We must admit, "God, I have no power. I deny my ability to deliver myself. I deny that I can crucify myself or have any power over sin. I give up all my own efforts to die to sin!"

By faith, we are "in Christ" -- and now we are to enjoy the benefits of all he has accomplished. You see, from the very moment we were born again, we have been in Christ -- and that means we entered into everything that happened to Christ, including all of his victories, as well as his crucifixion. So, if we agree with God's word that our sins are exceedingly wicked, we must also agree with the good things the cross offers as well. They are ours -- because Jesus accomplished them all for us!

For instance, God's word says that once we embrace the cross, we are crucified with Christ -- and we are resurrected with him into newness of life. Sin no longer has any dominion over us. We can do all things through Christ's strength. We are set free. We can yield our bodies to the service of the Lord and offer our members as instruments of righteousness.

At times you may stumble through all this, because of unbelief. But you can hold onto the truth that ultimately victory is yours -- because you cry, "Lord, I'm going to trust you until victory comes!"

I thank God for the cross of Christ -- and I thank God for its crisis. I know by experience that the greatest "grace preaching" in the world is the preaching of the cross!

And so, I ask you: Have you had your crisis of the cross? What about your present sinful condition? What about that one stronghold you long to be delivered from?

There is deliverance for you today. But it won't come until you kneel before Jesus and have your crisis at his cross. Only at the cross is there finality of sin. It is there you must agree with his word: "I can no longer continue in my sin, not for another hour. Oh, God, I'm weary of it. I bring it to you now!"

Paul lets us into a powerful insight in his letter to the Romans: "We know that our old self was crucified with him in order that the body of sin might be brought to nothing, so that we would no longer be enslaved to sin." (Romans 6:6) Firstly he says, "We know that our old self was crucified with him" – how do we know? We know it because God tells us in his word – and God cannot lie. Your old sinful flesh was crucified. When? At the same time Jesus was. Just as sure as Jesus died, so did you – you died with him. This is a positional truth, an established spiritual reality. When sinful desires arise, remind yourself that they have no power over you because you died with Christ. A corpse can't be tempted to sin.

Paul then goes on to say: "So you also must consider yourselves dead to sin and alive to God in Christ Jesus." (Rom. 6:11) So, you must know first, then consider. This is the application. Know that your flesh has been crucified, and therefore you are free from sins power – and therefore you must now consider this a fact. When sin comes knocking on your door simply point to the cross – a dead man can't sin.

Instead, we are to live in the power of the risen life that's within our spirits.

This is how we can overcome sin, not in our own strength but by the Spirit, and by faith in the finished work of the cross.

Yes, there may be times when we fail, and when we do we must confess our sins, repent of them and receive cleansing by the blood of Jesus and we must then rise up and walk in the victory that Christ has provided.

As the Lion of Judah roars, and the awakening call is heard throughout the globe – God is calling his crucified ones to arise. Arise as those who are dead to sin but alive in Christ. Arise as those who have died to personal ambition and ego. Arise as those who have died to pride, and respectability. Arise as those who manifest the risen Christ: Christ in us the hope of glory. As the army of crucified ones arise, so too shall the glory of Christ. Hell has nothing on this army. Satan has no foothold. This army will move in mighty resurrection power because it is not driven by human motivation, it is driven by the wind of God. Let the crucified warriors arise!

"...the Spirit comes to us as a fire, either to be fanned into full flame and given the freedom to accomplish his will or to be doused and extinguished by the water of human fear, control, and flawed theology."

Sam Storms, Practicing the Power: Welcoming the Gifts of the Holy Spirit in Your Life

10. Restoring the Gifts

Some people's conversion to Christianity is incredibly simple. They get converted within a particular group and they remain within that group for the rest of their lives, they never question the group's teachings, they just plug in and stay in. Some folks get saved in charismatic circles, and some get saved in non-charismatic circles, and both types will just embrace the teaching of the church where they met Jesus. That's not how it's worked for me.

I met with Jesus in a powerful and life changing way in 1999 as a result of hearing the gospel in a small brethren hall in Paisley. The group were faithful bible-believing Christians who loved Jesus but were wary of charismatic teaching (although there were more than a few closet charismatics within their ranks). The experience I had with God was not typical of what went on these church circles. Consequently, I would keep quiet about some of the experiences I was having following my conversion.

For example, one night I was reading the Bible into the small hours of the morning and an intense burning sensation fell upon me – it was terrifying. I immediately fell to my knees and cried out to God in very deep repentance – immediately following this I was overwhelmed with the purest joy I had ever experienced in my life.

The outcome of this experience was a very deep consciousness of the fear of the Lord. In hindsight, I think this may have been my initial baptism in the Spirit. Whilst I had been converted some several months prior to this, and whilst I had experienced the presence of God as a result of asking Jesus Christ into my life as Lord and saviour – this encounter was on a totally different level.

I had come to Christ as an 18 year old who had spent the last four years in an intense binge of narcotics and alcohol. My head was fried. I had left school with very poor qualifications and I had no aspirations aside from cashing my fortnightly benefit cheque from the Social Security office. Jesus changed all of that.

Whilst I had encountered Jesus, I still wasn't fully free. The narcotics weren't an issue, I stopped them easily enough. The drinking and smoking was another matter. I smoked around 20 cigarettes a day and I'd drink every day if I could. Despite this encounter with Jesus, I couldn't break free.

In the months that followed, I discovered a book by A.W. Tozer called 'How to be filled with the Holy Spirit'. In a nutshell the book teaches the importance of repentance, fresh surrender, and yielding to the Holy Spirit to the point that he is the one in charge of your life. In connection with the previous chapter – It was here I discovered that the Christian life was not about me living for Christ, but it was instead Christ living through me – by his Holy Spirit. This was life-changing.

First I experienced deliverance from addiction, and secondly the closeness of God's presence became a daily reality.

Yet there was more to be experienced. In the early hours of Pentecost Sunday 2000, as we entered the new millennium, I found myself lying in bed praying in a language I hadn't learned and a blanket of peace rested upon me. I was concerned by the fact that I could not understand the language – for this reason many in my church circles had argued against the gift, assuming that true tongues was a language that could be understood. Earnest for Biblical guidance, I picked up my Bible from the bedside table, and turned to 1 Corinthians 14: "For one who speaks in a tongue speaks not to men but to God; for no one understands him, but he utters mysteries in the Spirit." (1 Cor. 14:2)

All of a sudden it seemed clear – tongues were a means of speaking directly to God in a language that cannot be understood – unless accompanied by the gift of interpretation. The claim that 'Biblical tongues' had to be a language that could be understood did not line up with Paul's teaching in 1 Cor. 14. If the language had to be an earthly language – why would there always be a need for supernatural interpretation? Of course tongues can't be understood – that is what Paul teaches, the one praying in tongues is expressing mysteries through the Spirit of God.

As a young Christian I devoured the scriptures and any Christian book that I could get my hands on. I soon discovered that there was a major division in the Bible-believing evangelical streams of Christianity. Or to put it in the language of R.T. Kendall, there has been a great divorce. Kendall puts it this way (and it is worth quoting in full).

> Our premise is this. It seems to us that there has been a 'silent divorce' in the church, speaking generally, between the Word and the Spirit. When there is a divorce, some children stay with the mother, some stay with the father.
>
> In this divorce, there are those on the 'word' side and those on the 'Spirit' side. What is the difference?
>
> Take those of us who represent the Word. Our message is this: we must earnestly contend for the faith 'once delivered unto the saints' (Jude 3), we need get back to expository preaching, sound doctrine such as justification by faith, the sovereignty of God and the internal testimony of the Spirit as taught by men like Martin Luther, John Calvin and Jonathan Edwards. What is wrong with this emphasis? Nothing. It is exactly right.
>
> Take those whose emphasis has been on the Holy Spirit. What is the message? We need to rediscover the power that was manifested in the Book of Acts, there needs to be a demonstration of signs, wonders and miracles; we need to see the gifts of the Spirit operating in the church – that the world will once again take notice of the church so that people are left without excuse. What is wrong with this emphasis? Nothing. It is exactly right.

We believe that the need of the hour is not one or the other – but both! It is our view that this simultaneous combination will result in spontaneous combustion! And then, but almost certainly only then, will the world be shaken once again by the message of the church.

This was the message I have preached over the years at Westminster Chapel in London. This is what we are endeavouring to preach in America and around the world. This is not all we preach but it is certainly one of the main things we preach alongside the need for total forgiveness and learning to be sensitive to the voice of the Holy Spirit. We need your prayers. God bless you. Thank you for taking the time to read this special letter to you!

– Dr. R.T. Kendall[18]

Those who accept the truth of this 'Word and Spirit' tension often refer to themselves as 'Word and Spirit' people – some use other terms like 'Reformed Continuationist' or 'Evangelical-charismatic'. The idea behind the labels being that there is a group of believers that are committed to both the authority of scripture and the presence and gifts of the Holy Spirit.

As I mentioned at the start – some believers spend their lives in one camp or the other blissfully unaware of the tensions. In some respects it would be easier to be in one camp or the other – there would be no conflict. Everything would be tidier. But that's not the reality.

---

[18] http://rtkendallministries.com/about (Accessed 25/01/18).

It's a scandal that many believers have had to make a choice between faithfulness to sound doctrine and the scriptures or faithfulness to the presence and gifts of the Spirit.

For myself, I've spent most of my Christian life in non-denominational-pentecostal circles. This is where I felt most at home. That being said, I was always troubled by the lack of expository preaching, diminishing emphasis on scriptural authority, the lack of gospel clarity, a view of God that was half-baked and only focused on his love, and an approach to church government that was cooked up in some US business seminar. Consequently, as a result of these concerns, for a period of seven years, I leaned more towards the reformed wing of the church. I pastored two conservative churches for a short period of time, and I became a ministry candidate within a conservative Presbyterian denomination.

One of the things I discovered is that God isn't limited by denominational rules or doctrines. Within this conservative denomination – who on paper would be 'cessationist' there are a number of ministers, leaders, and members who believe in and who have experienced the gifts of the Holy Spirit, including speaking in tongues and prophecy. In fact, just last week one of the leaders from this denomination phoned me up because he wanted to discuss the things of the Spirit and finds that he is alone within his denomination. He has the gift of tongues, he believes in all the gifts, and he wants to see the power of God come upon his church in a deeper way – but he's restricted by the culture of the denomination.

I totally empathise with his situation. For a number of years, whilst I was in that denomination, I 'shelved' the gifts of the Spirit. I didn't outright reject them, but I just gave them a slightly different emphasis. I thought I could be faithful to my calling if I simply focused on preaching the gospel, and expounding the scriptures (conveniently not stressing the scriptures about the gifts and the miracles.) The problem is, God doesn't work like that. Where there are people genuinely hungry for God, the Spirit of God will always break through, no matter what our church creeds say.

There is a prophetic edge to my calling, I wouldn't call myself a prophet, but there is a prophetic edge. The more I push into God, the sharper this edge becomes. As a preacher in this conservative denomination, and whilst pastoring a small struggling church, I began to push in to God in prayer and crying out for an outpouring of the Spirit. In this situation, what I've discovered is that God is no respecter of doctrinal creeds. His presence will fall – if we want him. I've also discovered that it is possible for the gifts (at least some of the gifts) to function without the charismatic packaging. What do I mean?

Preaching, when carried out under the inspiration of the Spirit, can be a form of prophecy. There were many times I found myself departing from my notes as I was carried by the Spirit, and suddenly I would find myself addressing particular issues.

It wasn't dressed up in the language of "thus saith the Lord" (New Testament prophecy shouldn't be) but it was prophetic. I recall one visitor – a man who was months away from death, and who was not a Christian, shaking at the end of a service. "How did he do that?" he asked those in the chairs next to him. "How was he able to speak directly to me?" The people smiled – "Oh he didn't do that. That's the Lord speaking to you!"

Again, the gift of healing can function in our church services without the charismatic show that we often like to create. Two incidents come to mind, one was when I called for the elders to join with me in laying hands on one of the elders' wives. She was in chronic pain. The doctor said it would be months before she could expect any improvement. She has already been in this condition for months. As we laid hands on her, I felt something shift in her back. The next morning, I received a wonderful text about how she had experienced her first night's sleep in a long time – and that she has wakened up with no back pain. The pain never returned, and she testified in church the very next Sunday.

On another occasion, we prayed and laid hands on a lady after the service. The woman was grieving the loss of her daughter. The daughter had died a year before. The following Sunday she approached me with tears in her eyes, "John, I think you have the gift of healing," she said. She continued, "I've been unable to pick up a photo of my daughter and look at it without crying in distress.

After you prayed last Sunday, I went home and for the first time I was able to pick up her picture, and look at it without breaking down." Again, a wonderful example of the Lord's healing touch.

On another occasion, I was asked to take some services for a couple of churches in the highlands – Lairg. We discovered in that wonderful place some people who had experienced a move of the Holy Spirit a number of years' prior. A number of them had been filled with the Spirit and had received the gift of tongues. There had been a wonderful stirring of the Spirit, "until" one lady said, "One of the denominational leaders rode up here on his motorbike and shut it all down." The lady had been most unimpressed – she had continually asked the man "can you explain why these things are in the Bible, and why we have experienced them and why you are telling us to stop it from happening?"

"We just don't do these things. It's not our way." So that was that. It was shut down.

I'm conscious that I'm painting two pictures here. On the one hand, renewal of the gifts of the Spirit can happen even in the most conservative of denominations; however, there will often be a limit. Usually tongues are a step too far! If the Spirit begins to flow a little too freely, the denominational temple police will arrive at some point – unless there is a deep renewal at the heart of the denomination's leadership, most grassroots renewals will be short-lived.

One final example: in my latter time with this denomination I was part of a city centre church plant that was led by one of the denomination's more evangelistic leaders. He had a reputation for being used in revival, and he was much more open to the Spirit than many of the other leaders. Towards the end of the service, I sensed the Lord give a word of knowledge about someone who had experienced betrayal, and as a result was struggling with feelings of bitterness. After the service a woman shot towards me. It turned out that she had been betrayed by a good friend just that week and she was really struggling. She stood there physically shaking because the prophetic word had really gripped her. We prayed, I laid hands on her, and she began to quietly speak in tongues. She was shocked: "That's the first time I've prayed in tongues for a very long time!" She was glowing.

Immediately after this, an older gentleman came and spoke to me: "You need to plant a pentecostal work in Stirling." He wasn't an elder giving me the right foot of fellowship. It was a Pentecostal brother who felt the Lord had told him this is what I was to do. Interestingly, I had been speaking at a revival meeting the day before, and I had been speaking with some Pentecostal pastors about this very thing. Within a few months, my wife and I were prayed for, blessed and released by the leadership to go and pioneer a fresh work in the area.

One of the lessons I have taken from this experience is the fact that the gifts of the Spirit are essential for the well-being of the church. Prophecy is not just for encouragement, correction or direction – it is also for healing. How many of our church members are currently staggering around like the walking wounded? The prophetic ministry of the Spirit is given for their healing. There is something very precious about a "now" Word from the Lord that speaks to you at your deepest point of need.

In drawing this chapter to a conclusion, I very much feel that this book is a prophetic word. The Spirit is literally carrying me through several chapters a day. Other than the chapter headings, I have no plan. I'm quite surprised at the shape this chapter has taken – I thought it might be more exegetical or even more historical. Instead the Lord has led me to share from experience. There are many other experiences with the gifts that I could share, but let me just finish with one more word of encouragement.

I believe the Lord is calling is to deep prayer in this season, and as part of that it is important to stir up the gift of tongues. Paul writes: "What am I to do? I will pray with my spirit, but I will pray with my mind also; I will sing praise with my spirit, but I will sing with my mind also." (1 Cor. 14:15) When Paul uses the phrase "pray with my spirit" he is referring to praying in tongues.

This is contrasted with praying with his "mind" which he equates with praying with his natural language – a language he understands.

Praying with our spirit is a different ball game all together. As we pray with our spirit, we pray prophetically – remember, tongues when interpreted equates to prophecy. There is a different dimension at work when we pray in tongues – praying in tongues is warfare praying. Strongholds are demolished as we pray with our spirit.

This chapter is called restoring the gifts – it is not just the cessationist churches that need the gifts restored, many of our 'Spirit-filled' churches need a restoration of the gifts. Many have lost their way. Some struggle to pray for more than a minute in the spirit. We should be more equipped than this. God is calling us to step up higher and to move in deeper. As the lion roars – he is awakening our spirits to roar with him. As our spirits roar with prayer and praise, the forces of darkness are driven back as the kingdom comes forth with power.

"At the name of Aslan each one of the children felt something jump in its inside. Edmund felt a sensation of mysterious horror. Peter felt suddenly brave and adventurous. Susan felt as if some delicious smell or some delightful strain of music had just floated by her. And Lucy got the feeling you have when you wake up in the morning and realize that it is the beginning of the holidays or the beginning of summer."

C.S. Lewis, The Lion, the Witch and the Wardrobe

11. Worshipping the Lion-Like Lamb

What should worship look like? If we were to look at how the various churches worship, we would arrive at one conclusion – or perhaps just arrive at confusion! However, if we were to look at examples of worship in scripture, I think we would arrive at a very different conclusion. Think about some of the worship scenes in scripture – think of John's Revelation, or Daniel's spiritual encounter, or think of Moses before the burning bush, or even Isaiah as he receives a revelation of the Lord – what language would we use to describe these worship encounters? Awesome? Majestic? Fearful? Intense?

Now think about the words we might use to describe what happens in many churches on the average Sunday morning. Predictable? Boring? Bland? Funeral-like? Austere? Shallow? Hyped up? Suppressed?

Annie Dillard put her finger on the problem when she penned these prophetic, and provocative words:

> On the whole, I do not find Christians, outside of the catacombs, sufficiently sensible of conditions. Does anyone have the foggiest idea what sort of power we so blithely invoke? Or, as I suspect, does no one believe a word of it?

> The churches are children playing on the floor with their chemistry sets, mixing up a batch of TNT to kill a Sunday morning. It is madness to wear ladies' straw hats and velvet hats to church; we should all be wearing crash helmets. Ushers should issue life preservers and signal flares; they should lash us to our pews.[19]

Wow. Those words never fail to impact me. It's clear she understands something of the nature of God and something of the way that our typical church services are so far removed from anything that remotely reflects a consciousness of who we are actually worshipping.

Charismatics and Pentecostals are not off the hook here – just because we may understand something of the importance of the anointing does not mean that we are any better than our conservative brethren. Tommy Tenney hits the nail on the head:

> The anointing may make us worship or preach better, but we need to remember that the anointing—whether it falls on us individually or on a congregation during a service—is not the end, but just the beginning. Some would prostitute the anointing by "dancing around in front of the veil" of God's presence, not realizing that its whole purpose is to prepare them to enter in, to go past the veil into His glory. The King's chamber, the Holy of Holies, awaits the anointed.

---

[19] *Annie Dillard*, Teaching a Stone to Talk, *58*.

> The Word of God tells us that the veil of division was torn in two by Jesus Christ's death on Calvary, and that we have free entry into God's presence through the blood of Jesus. We just aren't entering in. Occasionally somebody falls or stumbles his way past the veil during our dancing sessions and then comes back with a wild-eyed stare. But we usually go back into our dancing mode right in front of the veil.
>
> We get all excited about the possibility but we never really consummate the process. The purpose of the anointing is to help us make the transition from flesh into glory. One reason we like to linger in the anointing is that it makes the flesh feel good. On the other hand, when the glory of God comes, the flesh doesn't feel very comfortable. When the glory of God comes, we become like the prophet Isaiah. Our flesh is so weakened by His presence that it is unnecessary for man to do anything other than behold Him in His glory.[20]

Tommy's challenge is relevant for every Bible-believing Christian – the sole purpose of Jesus shedding his blood is that we may enter into the very throne room of God. Yet how many of us stand at the threshold? The blood has been shed, and the veil in the old temple was torn in two, from top to bottom. God himself has removed the barrier – but if we are honest we don't really want to get too close. We prefer God at a distance.

---

[20] Tenney, Tommy, *God Chasers*, p41-43.

There is an old worship song that expresses this desire to meet God in the most Holy Place.

> Take me past the outer courts into the holy place
> Past the brazen altar, Lord, I want to see your face
> Pass me by the crowds of people, the
> Priest who sing your praise
> I hunger and thirst for your righteousness
> But it's only found one place
>
> Take me in to the holy of hollies
> Take me in by the blood of the lamb
> Take me in to the holy of hollies
> Take the coal, touch my lips, here I am

These are wonderful words that mingle Isaiah's experience with the New Covenant revelation that we can enter God's presence by the blood of the lamb. I've mentioned the Isaiah experience a few times; let us now turn to that passage.

> In the year that King Uzziah died I saw the Lord sitting upon a throne, high and lifted up; and the train of his robe filled the temple. Above him stood the seraphim. Each had six wings: with two he covered his face, and with two he covered his feet, and with two he flew. And one called to another and said:
> "Holy, holy, holy is the Lord of hosts; the whole earth is full of his glory!"

> And the foundations of the thresholds shook at the voice of him who called, and the house was filled with smoke. And I said: "Woe is me! For I am lost; for I am a man of unclean lips, and I dwell in the midst of a people of unclean lips; for my eyes have seen the King, the Lord of hosts!"
>
> Then one of the seraphim flew to me, having in his hand a burning coal that he had taken with tongs from the altar. And he touched my mouth and said: "Behold, this has touched your lips; your guilt is taken away, and your sin atoned for."

(Isaiah 6:1-7)

It's impossible to read this account and not feel the power and holiness which radiates from Isaiah's encounter with the Lord. Isaiah is awe-struck, and so should we be. Many Christians assume that New Covenant has put an end to the fear of the Lord as an aspect of worship. They could not be more wrong. Let us turn to the New Testament vision of worship.

> [5] And one of the elders said to me, "Weep no more; behold, the Lion of the tribe of Judah, the Root of David, has conquered, so that he can open the scroll and its seven seals."
>
> [6] And between the throne and the four living creatures and among the elders I saw a Lamb standing, as though it had been slain, with seven horns and with seven eyes, which are the seven spirits of God sent out into all the earth. (Rev 5:5-6)

The apostle John, like Isaiah and Daniel before him is awe-struck by his revelation of Christ. The exalted Christ is revealed as both the lion and the lamb – he is both Saviour and Lord. Yes he is full of love and grace, but oh he is a terrifying and reigning king – he is the Lion of the tribe of Judah.

In C.S. Lewis' classic, 'the Lion, the Witch, and the Wardrobe, there is a scene where young Lucy asks Mr Beaver if Aslan, the Lion, is safe. Mr Beaver replies: "Safe? Who said anything about safe? 'Course he isn't safe. But he's good. He's the King."

I wonder if there would be more awestruck worshippers if we had a stronger revelation of Jesus the Lamb-like Lion?

Having served in more mainstream churches in the last few years, and often having responsibility for shaping the order of worship within a number of churches, I became deeply aware that worship is an area that is deeply under attack. This is especially the case where traditional congregations are attempting to transition towards a more contemporary expression of worship. I've experienced these tensions first-hand, and I know the 'worship wars' are affecting churches all over the world. Sadly many Christians are blind to the devil's tactics, they are so consumed by their own desires when it comes to worship that they fail to see how the devil is using the worship wars to divide the church and destroy worship.

This is one of the reasons why I knew that I could no longer continue to help build these kind of congregations, if a congregation is not united in something as foundational as worship – it will be impossible for that church to grow into the full stature of Christ that is described in Ephesians 4. As Jesus said, 'a house divided cannot stand.'

Terry Virgo touches on this problem and notes that some have even suggested that,

> God developed different denominations with their different styles of worship in order that we could select one that reflects our preference and suits our temperament. All extraverts can join the Pentecostals, while more sober believers can settle elsewhere. What a tragic misunderstanding of God's purpose.[21]

What is even more tragic than denominations divided by temperament, is when believers begin to cross-pollinate, and denominations try to evolve, and the local congregations are divided by competing factions. This is the tragic reality amongst far too many churches today – and the battle can be seen in both non-charismatic and charismatic churches.

Terry Virgo addresses the issue effectively:

> God is seeking those who will worship him "in Spirit and in truth", not in temperament and preference.

---

[21] Virgo, Terry, The Spirit-Filled Church, p71.

In God's glorious kingdom extraverts will learn to be hushed in awe before Him and those formally inhibited will be drunk with new wine.[22]

As an itinerant preacher, I have travelled throughout Scotland preaching the gospel, and as I have done so, I have often feared that much of what we do as church is carried out on our own strength. We are so busy ministering *for* the Lord that we have ceased to minister *to* the Lord. We have made church all about us, rather than all about him. We see this haunting scenario in one of the churches in the book of Revelation.

To the church in Laodicea, Jesus says: "Here I am! I stand at the door and knock. If anyone hears my voice and opens the door, I will come in and eat with that person, and they with me." (Rev. 3:20)

Here was a church, doing all the things that churches do, possibly singing with gusto, "I surrender all" and whilst all this is going on, amidst the noise of church, there was a faint knocking at the door. Did anyone hear it?

Were there no prophets in the midst? What were they saying? Were the prophets standing up saying: 'Behold the Lord is in our midst doing a new thing. Behold he is here with us this morning!"? Yet the reality is, the Lord was on the outside – locked out of his own church.

---

[22] Virgo, Spirit-filled, p71.

Woe to the prophets who prophesy lies. It is the prophets who should be hearing the knocking at the door. It is the prophets who should be standing up and saying: "open up the doors and let the King of Glory come in!" Prophets are doorkeepers! Prophets hold the keys – God will hold the prophets accountable – will we go along with show, just having a good time – working up religious zeal – or will we speak the truth? Will we tell the church the truth – we've pushed Jesus to the outskirts – and he's knocking at the door. Will we let him in? Will we give him his rightful place? The Lord wants his church back, and he's standing at the door and knocking.

As I was preparing this manuscript, I was hesitating about including a chapter on worship. Just at that moment, I was tagged in the following prophetic post which was shared by Kenny Borthwick. It confirmed to me that I needed to include a chapter on worship. Here is the word that Kenny shared:

It is possible to miss the moment. I remember a dream I had in the 90's in which Renewal of God's Purposes in Scotland was represented in the form of a lion. The lion walked into one of the biggest churches in the city. The congregation fled and only returned when the lion left. They picked up their hymn books and started to sing at exactly the point they had been at before the lion came.

Meanwhile the lion moved on to other more welcoming gatherings. The moment of renewal in that confident church was missed, indeed fled from, in favour of "no change, business as usual!"

I am not suggesting Coronavirus represents God renewing the Church, but it would be really sad if we all picked up our hymn books and sang from where we left off as it were once this is over, as though that somehow represented faithfulness that merits a pat on our backs from ourselves. This really is a season when new things can blossom that maybe would not otherwise have come about. Of course there are those who wax in learned tones as to why we should not change this or that as though a change represents a denial of our heritage.

Have the courage, humility and joy not to be one of those voices nor to pay greater homage to them however illustrious than to the Word and Spirit of God. Sometimes aspects of our heritage need to be left behind in favour of a truer faithfulness to the Christ of Scripture rather than the Christ of a particular theology, or the practices of a particular time that were perhaps one way of being faithful to Christ at a given moment, but not the only way for all time.

In Kenny's picture – the lion visited the church and he was not welcome – the church wanted business as usual.

I'm saying that the current shake up that's happened because of the Coronavirus is God getting our attention.

The Lion is roaring, but are we listening? Will we respond to his call? It is a call to worship. It's a call to leave behind all that restricts us. We must be willing to lay aside the cold traditions of men and respond to the Lion's call. It's time for the worshippers to arise.

"The second coming of Christ will be so revolutionary that it will change every aspect of life on this planet. Christ will reign in righteousness. Disease will be arrested. Death will be modified. War will be abolished. Nature will be changed. Man will live as it was originally intended he should live."

Billy Graham, Billy Graham in Quotes

"The first time, Christ came to slay sin in men. The second time, He will come to slay men in sin."

A. W. Pink

12. A Vision of the Return of Christ

He's coming on the clouds, kings and kingdoms will bow down…Our God is the Lion, the Lion of Judah, He's roaring with power and fighting our battles, And every knee will bow before You, Our God is the Lamb, the Lamb that was slain, For the sin of the world, His blood breaks the chains, And every knee will bow before the Lion and the Lamb.
Big Daddy Weave

The King is coming; it's time to get ready!

If the Covid19 pandemic has taught me anything it is this: we need to wake up because the Lord's return is drawing near. Many of us have become like five foolish virgins who ran out of oil – when the midnight cry came, they were unprepared. Most of us were unprepared for this virus. We were certainly unprepared for a global lockdown. Yet SUDDENLY it came upon us. This is the Lord's way of waking us up. More than ever we need to prepare our hearts and lives – the king is coming.

There was a time when the thought of the Lord's return would fill me with dread. I guess it was because I lacked assurance of salvation. Now however, things are different, the thought of the Lord's return fills me with joy. And this is how it should affect all believers. Jesus told is to look for the signs of the times, but he also told us how we should respond when we do see them.

"And there will be signs in sun and moon and stars, and on the earth distress of nations in perplexity because of the roaring of the sea and the waves, people fainting with fear and with foreboding of what is coming on the world. For the powers of the heavens will be shaken. And then they will see the Son of Man coming in a cloud with power and great glory. Now when these things begin to take place, straighten up and raise your heads, because your redemption is drawing near." (Luke 21:25-28)

Now is not the time for complacency. Now is the time to press into the "secret place", now is the time to get rid of any sin, now is the time for intercession and now is the time for bold proclamation of the gospel.

I'll be honest, I've been a Christian for around 20 years, and for most of that time, the return of Christ has not been a major emphasis. I have, in my preaching and teaching, attempted to be faithful to the Bible. When I pastored churches, I took them through books of the Bible. My first sermon, in one church, was on Acts chapter one – this naturally led to preaching on the second coming. But by and large, it's not been an emphasis.

However, in recent days, I think this may have been a mistake. Perhaps my reluctance to focus too much on the End Times has been an over-reaction to the dispensational teaching I encountered as a new believer in the brethren churches.

Maybe some of the eschatological scepticism that is characteristic of the reformed churches has rubbed off on me. Whatever the reason, I'm keen to address that imbalance – not by over-emphasis, but by correct emphasis. The Lord's return is one of the most repeated themes in scripture. All other doctrines should be held in view of the Lord's return. Yes, all other doctrines.

When we lose sight of the Lord's return, there is a tendency to become immersed in the here and now. No wonder we don't think evangelism is urgent when we are living our lives only thinking about the here and now. No wonder our worship lacks majesty and awe when most of the time we think of the cross without seeing the cross in the broader context of his resurrection, ascension and return.

Maybe we need to go back to reciting the apostles' creed in our churches – the creed which takes us through the God-head, to the incarnation, to the death, resurrection, ascension and second coming of the Lord. That gets read every week in Anglican and Catholic churches. (That's not to say it's 'heard' every week. I heard it every week as a young Catholic and was none the wiser to what it actually meant!)

How would our church life be transformed, if everything we did was connected to the bigger picture of the Lord's return? How does the Lord's return affect evangelism? Surely it should motivate us to bring in the harvest. It should inform our gospel message – "repent, for the kingdom of heaven is at hand – the King is coming!"

How could the second coming enrich our discipleship? Perhaps as a reminder of what it is all about – preparing the Bride for the Lord's return. Discipleship is about getting ready to meet Jesus.

How would affect our attitude to sin? Perhaps we would take grace much less for granted, perhaps we would sin less readily if we regularly reminded ourselves that the Judge of all the earth is coming soon – be ready.

How might it affect our prayer life? Surely it fills our prayers with both earnestness and joy!

How might it affect our pastoral care or marriage counselling? Greatly! Husbands and wives – does your present conflict really matter in the light of his coming? Is this squabble worth divorcing over? Is this what you want to be doing when Jesus returns? Husband, is that adulterous affair really what you want to be doing? How will you feel about it on the day of his return? Will you not be filled with shame and regret?

How might a fresh emphasis on the Lord's return help us overcome discouragement and even depression? Greatly! The Lord's return is our great hope. When everything in this world seems dark, when sin is on the increase, when injustice seems to rule the day, when the church is marginalised, and when we are battling our own sinful hearts – what can give us hope? Christ is coming soon! And on that day justice shall flow like a river.

> See what kind of love the Father has given to us, that we should be called children of God; and so we are. The reason why the world does not know us is that it did not know him. Beloved, we are God's children now, and what we will be has not yet appeared; but we know that when he appears[g] we shall be like him, because we shall see him as he is. And everyone who thus hopes in him purifies himself as he is pure.
>
> *(1 John 3:1-3)*

When we fix our eyes on the Lord's return, we purify ourselves in preparation. When we neglect to reflect on his return, we may become complacent, and compromise. As a result we are unprepared for his return. Friend, are you ready for the Lord's return? Or will that day come as a traumatic shock? Are there things in your life that you know you would be ashamed of if Jesus were to return right now?

It's time to seek the Lord for deliverance – there is fresh oil flowing from heavens courts – the oil will meet your every need. Oil is the need of the hour. Oil speaks of the Holy Spirit and the anointing. Remember the parable that Jesus taught:

> "Then the kingdom of heaven shall be likened to ten virgins who took their lamps and went out to meet the bridegroom. ² Now five of them were wise, and five *were* foolish.
>
> ³ Those who *were* foolish took their lamps and took no oil with them, ⁴ but the wise took oil in their vessels with their lamps.
>
> ⁵ But while the bridegroom was delayed, they all slumbered and slept.

⁶ "And at midnight a cry was *heard:* 'Behold, the bridegroom is coming; go out to meet him!' ⁷ Then all those virgins arose and trimmed their lamps. ⁸ And the foolish said to the wise, 'Give us *some* of your oil, for our lamps are going out.' ⁹ But the wise answered, saying, '*No,* lest there should not be enough for us and you; but go rather to those who sell, and buy for yourselves.' ¹⁰ And while they went to buy, the bridegroom came, and those who were ready went in with him to the wedding; and the door was shut.

¹¹ "Afterward the other virgins came also, saying, 'Lord, Lord, open to us!' ¹² But he answered and said, 'Assuredly, I say to you, I do not know you.'

¹³ "Watch therefore, for you know neither the day nor the hour in which the Son of Man is coming.

(Matt 25:1-3)

This passage is a warning for the church. All of them were virgins – this means that they were all followers of Christ. Virginity represents purity. Only those who have come to Christ for forgiveness are pure. However, they neglected to take care of their lamps. What are our lamps? It is our witness. Our walk with Christ. We are called to let our light shine. These professing believers were negligent. They were not depending on the Lord. They lacked oil – in other words, they lacked the Holy Spirit. They had been living on borrowed light from the other virgins. Perhaps when all ten were together, it was not so apparent that five of them were not shining, instead they were living on the benefits of other believers' lamps.

When the Bridegroom comes, we will not be able to lean on the faith of others. We will not be able to draw from other believers' supply. On that Day we will be exposed for who we really are.

Make no mistake, now, and not later, is the time to get ready. Now is the time to seek the Lord. Now is the time to get your house in order.

The Lion of Judah is roaring with a mighty roar. It's a call to get ready. It's a trumpet blast. It's a wake up cry! If you get ready now, you will be prepared for the final trumpet blast when the Lord appears in glory.

For the Lord himself will descend from heaven with a cry of command, with the voice of an archangel, and with the sound of the trumpet of God. And the dead in Christ will rise first. Then we who are alive, who are left, will be caught up together with them in the clouds to meet the Lord in the air, and so we will always be with the Lord. Therefore encourage one another with these words.

(1 Thess. 4:16-18)

ABOUT THE AUTHOR

John Caldwell is an itinerant preacher, author and school teacher who lives in Perthshire, Scotland, with his wife Laura and two sons Ethan and Caleb. Prior to entering the teaching profession, he worked for Paisley YMCA in a variety of projects that reached out to young people throughout Renfrewshire. John preaches and teaches across various churches, denominations and Christian gatherings across Scotland.

For more than 15 years, John has been assisting local churches, and Christian gatherings, throughout Scotland by sharing his testimony and preaching and teaching the Bible. John's Spirit-filled, Christ-centred and down-to-earth delivery is well-received by Christians and non-Christians alike.

John holds a BD (Hons) in Theology and Pastoral Studies from the Scottish Baptist College, a Post-Graduate Diploma in Education (Religious Education and English), he studied English Literature and Fiction Writing at the Open University, and he studied Youthwork and Theology at the International Christian College.

For 'down time' he loves camping with his wife, kids and dog in scenic Scotland.

For more info, or to contact John, visit: www.john-caldwell.com.

OTHER BOOKS BY JOHN CALDWELL

Many communities are ravaged by problems associated with poverty, crime and drug and alcohol abuse. Substantial answers to the urban crisis are all but non-existent. 'Christ, the Cross and the Concrete Jungle' is the story of a young man's deliverance from a lifestyle of desperation and delinquency to a new life of freedom and hope. This book reveals the remarkable journey of transformation and redemption that is made possible through the gospel of Jesus Christ.

Vision from the Valleys:

100 Daily Devotions Birthed out of the Welsh Revival and Apostolic Movement

John Caldwell's 'Vision from the Valleys' is a welcome addition to our understanding of what God did when he stirred the Welsh Revival into being in the first years of the twentieth century. Men and women, many with limited formal education, carried to their nation and the world a revelation of Christ and his Church which was fresh and deep in equal measure. Of course, each generation must discover the breath of God on truth, else the fresh becomes stale and the deep becomes shallow.

'Vision from the Valleys' takes us not to a moment in history, but allows us to glimpse into things eternal; 'Vision' takes us not to the Wales of a another era but to a setting into which for a season, at least, God's will was done on earth as in heaven.

May all who read be transported not back to a time and place now buried in history but propelled into a contemporary understanding and expression of God's love for the Church and his mission to reach all mankind with the Gospel. This is the heritage of the Apostolic Church, its mantle to help carry and its mission to help fulfil.

Tim Jack (National Leader, Apostolic Church, UK)

Printed in Great Britain
by Amazon